THE FIRST EMPEROR
OF CHINA

Frances Wood

P

PROFILE BOOKS

This paperback edition published in 2008

First published in Great Britain in 2007 by
Profile Books Ltd
3A Exmouth House
Pine Street
Exmouth Market
London ECIR OJH
www.profilebooks.com

1 3 5 7 9 10 8 6 4 2

Typeset in Garamond by MacGuru Ltd
info@macguru.org.uk
Printed and bound in Great Britain by
CPI Bookmarque, Croydon, CR0 4TD

A CIP catalogue record for this book is available from the British Library.

ISBN 978 1 84668 041 0

Mixed Sources
Product group from well-managed
forests and other controlled sources
www.fsc.org Cert no. TT-COC-002227
© 1996 Forest Stewardship Council
FSC

Contents

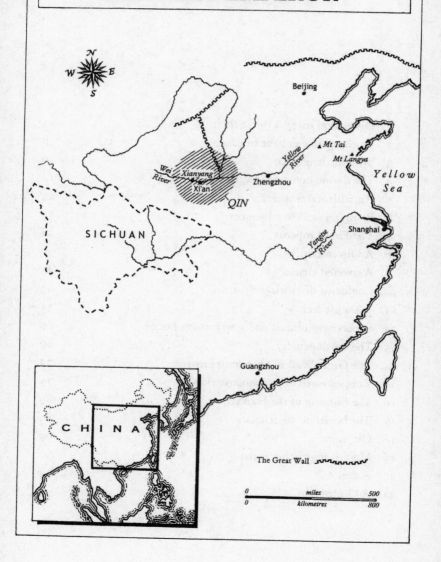

CHINA DURING THE REIGN OF
THE FIRST EMPEROR

Beijing

Mt Tai

Mt Langya

Yellow River

Wei River

Xianyang

Xi'an

QIN

Zhengzhou

Yellow Sea

SICHUAN

Yangtse River

Shanghai

CHINA

Guangzhou

The Great Wall

| 0 | miles | 500 |
| 0 | kilometres | 800 |

List of Illustrations

INTRODUCTION

Elephants, Steamed Duck and Warring States

The only reason that people outside the country know of the First Emperor of China (259–210 BC) is because a new well was required in Xiyang village, Yanzhai rural commune, Lintong county, Shaanxi province. In 1974, when digging their well, the villagers unearthed the terracotta soldiers of the 'Buried Army', part of the First Emperor's great tomb.

For the hundreds of thousands of tourists who now visit the Buried Army, the terracotta soldiers are more significant than the life of the man they were set to guard. In China, however, the significance of the First Emperor, as founder of imperial China and father of the imperial bureaucracy that governed its vast territories for 2,000 years (much to the admiration of Voltaire and Leibniz), is completely overshadowed by his notoriety. For the bureaucratic ruling class that he effectively created, he became a tyrannical bogeyman, the enemy of intellectual life and historic culture.

The future First Emperor of China was born in 259 BC, the eldest son and heir of the King of Qin (pronounced 'chin'). The state of Qin lay in the west, centred on the Wei River valley in today's Shaanxi province, though the First Emperor's ancestors are said to have moved eastwards from Gansu province. This 'external' origin, distant from the heartland further east, close to the Yellow River (near today's city of Zhengzhou), has prompted traditionalist Chinese archaeologists to declare the Qin a 'barbarian' state, with the implication that the First Emperor's legendary tyranny might have been a result of his non-Chinese origin.[1]

The Wei River, part of the great pattern of river arteries in China, cuts west to east through the dry loess or 'yellow earth' highlands before flowing into the Yellow River at the point where it turns east to run towards the sea. This 'yellow earth' is fine, wind-blown silt which, fortunately for local farmers, is capable of holding considerable moisture in an area of little rainfall. It is also easily cut, so many people lived in tunnel houses hollowed out of vertical loess cliffs.[2] Farming was mainly restricted to the river valleys.

Half a century before the birth of the First Emperor, the state of Qin had already begun to expand, conquering the state of Shu in Sichuan province and extending its control northwards into the upper bend of the Yellow River. The process of conquest continued under the First Emperor, who is described as having 'unified China' in 221 BC.

The area covered by the new empire stretched from just north of today's Beijing down to the northern borders of Guangdong province in the south, and from the northwards course of the Yellow River in Shaanxi and Sichuan provinces across to the eastern seaboard. The extent of the First Emperor's domains was huge when compared with that of his immediate predecessors.[3] More significantly and remarkably, China was to remain much the same in size and extent for centuries, though the Han dynasty extended their control out along the Gansu corridor, making contact with Central Asia and the Silk Road, and into Fujian and Guangdong. Not until the eighteenth century did the Qing emperors expand the country in an enormous programme of settlement northwards and westwards.

The earliest inhabitants of China, where settled agriculture began in about 5000 BC, have been characterized archaeologically by their locality, the agriculture they practised and their distinctive forms of pottery. Though they have until recently been classified into two main groups, archaeological finds continue to expand their numbers and geographical spread. Most of these communities, separated by mountain ranges and great rivers, must have been unaware of each other's existence and they developed individual characteristic cultural traits.

In the west, along the Wei River, were sites occupied by the millet-growing 'painted pottery' culture whose red clay burial urns were decorated with swirling patterns in black, and to the east was a culture whose pottery eventually developed into a form characterized by a burnished black surface and complex articulated shapes, unlike the curved forms of the painted pots. Further south, along the Yangtze River, local cultures produced cord-marked pottery and cultivated rice.[4] At some point there appears to have been an eastwards movement of the black pottery culture towards the centre, to what are now Henan and Shaanxi provinces. The appearance of tripod pottery forms (anticipating the tripods of the Bronze Age) and the production of carved jades indicate the significance of this particular culture in the subsequent development of characteristically Chinese artefacts.

According to traditional Chinese historiography, one of the great mythological creator figures, the 'Tamer of the Floods' who (temporarily) solved one of China's recurring problems by opening channels to the sea, thus preventing floods, was a ruler of the Xia dynasty. Despite suspicion about the existence of the Xia, first articulated by the 'Doubting Archaeology' school in the 1920s, archaeologists now tentatively ascribe a late site of the black pottery culture to the Xia, and the beginnings of the Bronze Age to about 1900 BC.[5]

Whether or not the Xia dynasty existed, it is clear that by the third millennium BC, there were numerous settled communities in China, scattered from west to east along the Wei and Yellow rivers into the Shandong peninsula and southwards from the Yellow River. This area, from the 'central plain' and eastwards, was the Chinese heartland. Many settlements were well-developed walled villages with ritual centres and separate graveyards.

According to traditional Chinese sources, the Xia was followed by the Shang dynasty (c. 1570–1045 BC). Archaeological discoveries in the early twentieth century set the Shang in the central plain along the Wei River and the middle Yellow River valley with their capital at Anyang. Shang culture was characterized by the use of bronze weapons and vessels, the latter cast in clay moulds and often displaying complex incised decoration. The Shang period is known not only from traditional histories but also from the writings left on inscribed ox bones and turtle shells known as 'oracle bones'. These were used by diviners to test the approval of proposed activities (hunting, for example, or warfare) by their gods and to try to foretell the outcome of illnesses or births. Some of the inscriptions, such as those referring to lunar eclipses, have been used to establish firm dates, but much of the material is best seen as providing only a relative guide to the period in which it was produced.[6]

卜稽如台圖

1. *Testing the views of the gods: divination using a turtle shell*

The extent of Shang domains is also difficult to assess but it seems clear that the major sites were concentrated in the central plain.[7] In 1045 BC, the Shang king was defeated in battle and the Zhou dynasty assumed power. Though there is considerable argument about the origin of the Zhou, by the time they seized control, they seem to have been settled to the west, in the area of the Wei River and its northern tributaries.[8] Maps of the Zhou domains, though tentative and based on traditional literature and archaeological evidence, show the same settlement in the central plain but with a great increase in the number of sites, following the course of the lower Yangtze and beyond.[9] With an enlarged area to control, the kings of Zhou chose to appoint nobles to rule over different regions, acts often commemorated in inscriptions cast on bronze vessels.[10] From the seventh century BC, this system gradually disintegrated as local rulers asserted their power and the Zhou domains became what has, rather inexactly, been termed a 'multi-state' system.[11]

By the fifth century BC, this situation of separation was such that the period 481–221 BC later became known as the 'Warring States period' in which the kings of the seven dominant states and their lesser rivals struggled for supremacy.[12] In this period, though the states of the middle and lower Yellow River remained the most significant, the middle and lower Yangtze River area was still important, extending Chinese rule southwards.

Through his conquest of all rival kings when he was a prince in the state of Qin, the First Emperor crushed the separatist states and in 221 BC unified the area from the Liaodong peninsula to Hainan Island. Thus, he brought all the separate and different cultures of the landmass, with their very different and separate histories, beliefs and artefacts, under his rule. These included the Sichuan plain, where great bronze cartwheels and elongated life-size bronze figures with mask-like faces, unlike anything seen from the Yellow River valley, have been unearthed at Sanxingdui;[13] the Zhongshan kingdom with its massive bronzes cast with complex knotted, tightly curled spirals; and the great kingdom of Chu with its shamans and weird wooden animistic gods with deer antlers and long red tongues. All were now part of a united empire.[14]

Despite great regional differences, China in 221 BC was an agrarian country, its agriculture dominated by the production of grain. Pigs and chickens were kept on farms, horses and oxen were used as draught animals, mainly in the north, and a few sheep were kept for wool, these being grazed on the field margins. There was no tradition of large flocks in China, although beyond the Great Wall, beyond China's borders to the north and north-west, the peoples of the grasslands were pastoralists.

The landscape looked very different to what it does today. Now, the central plain 'yellow earth' heartland, characterized by fine yellow soil, is very bare and, indeed, very yellow. During the Warring States period, however, and during the time of the First Emperor, it is likely that the hillsides would have been covered with scrub and that much more of the land, now intensively farmed, would have been covered with trees. Land was often cleared in the first instance to enable hunting to take place. The clearings in which horsemen were able to pursue forest animals were then taken over by farmers. Even as late as 120 BC there are reports of numerous elephants, tigers and rhinoceroses in the open forests beside the rivers that threaded their way across the north of China.

The Yellow River, which flowed around the central heartland, was only known as 'The River' to the First Emperor, partly because

2. Teaching an elephant to dance: from a Han dynasty tomb brick

of its significance in the area and partly because it was probably less loaded with yellow silt when the hillsides were still wooded and the grasslands had not yet been taken over for agriculture.[15] The central heartland was a warm temperate zone of deciduous broad-leafed trees where temperatures fell to below freezing in winter and rose to 26–28 degrees centigrade in summer. Rainfall was not heavy, particularly inland, which meant that 'dry-land farming' was a risky undertaking. Efforts to control the flow of 'The River' were made in the Warring States period, with levées built 10 kilometres back from the river bank to allow for seasonal flooding, but soon after the First Emperor's reign, farmers moved in to cultivate the rich alluvial deposits. With deforestation upstream and weakened defences, the Yellow River then began its long career of silting, flooding and changing course, gaining it the name of 'China's Sorrow'.[16]

The lands to the west and south that the First Emperor conquered offered rather different climates and conditions. In the warm, frost-free south and west, where rainfall was greater, tigers lurked in the forests. Here grew wonderful trees such as the camphor and the catalpa. However, with the arrival of iron axes in about 500 BC, deforestation had already begun to take place. The resulting timber, used to erect buildings of all sorts and sizes and to fire the kilns that produced pots, roof tiles, drain-pipes and, eventually, terracotta warriors for the First Emperor's Buried Army, was transported across the country by river and canal.

Water control was essential, not only to allow the movement of timber from one part of the country to another, but also to irrigate the fields and control flooding. When the First Emperor conquered the west, his territory included the irrigation network on the Min River, which can still be seen today. In order to irrigate the Sichuan plain, waterways were regularly dredged by a complex scheme of engineering bends. These directed the deposit of silt towards the slower flowing inner side of channels which could then be flushed out downstream. The channels were controlled by great bamboo baskets, perhaps three metres long and a metre in diameter, and filled with great round stones. These stone-filled baskets could be moved (with much difficulty and many labourers) as required.[17]

Another early irrigation and water-control scheme was a canal built when the First Emperor was still ruler of Qin, in 246 BC, in the central heartland. This took heavily silted water along a contour line to the Luo River and helped to combat the natural salinity of the soil, for along its upper reaches it released water into the fields, irrigating and fertilizing them and so helping to feed the growing population of the heartland and the First Emperor's capital. Shortly after the First Emperor's reign, the canal was described as contributing to the First Emperor's successful unification by transforming the alkaline soil and making the heartland fertile, so enabling his state to become 'rich and powerful'.[18] (The canal survived for about five hundred years, until one of its major feeder rivers gradually sank in its bed.[19]) A further canal system was created by the First Emperor

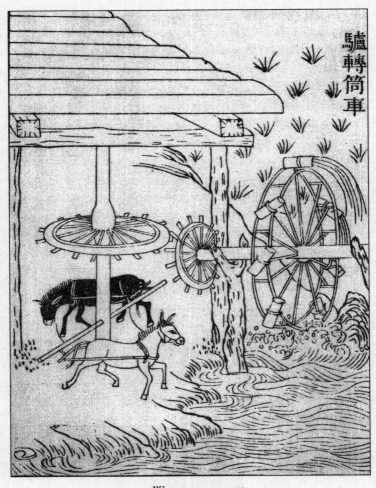

驢轉筒車

3. *Water management*

to transport grain and other supplies from the Yangtze River down to Guangzhou during his campaign in the south. Using rivers and a canal, it created an inland waterway system 2,000 kilometres long that is still in use today.[20]

During the Warring States period, farmers cultivated land assigned to them by local rulers, working in the fields with iron spades, sometimes forked in form, ox-drawn iron ploughs, hoes, rakes and sickles, and reaping knives.[21] There were rituals associated with the annual cycle of sowing, planting and harvesting, and the calendar, fixed by the ruler, established the cycle to be followed. In the dry north, it was not just timing but the method of sowing that was significant. To obtain maximum benefit from the moisture in the soil, seeds had to be sown in well-spaced, straight rows. In the wetter south, seeds could be broadcast, although rice was more carefully cultivated and transplanted for maximum cropping.[22]

There is some evidence that weeds were sometimes ploughed back into fields as 'green manure' although various animal by-products appear to have been more widely used. It seems likely that 'the combining of privies with pig-pens' was an early innovation, and though animals were not kept in large quantities, their manure was carefully collected and composted. The value of silk-worm droppings as fertilizer was mentioned as early as the first century BC.[23]

All rulers were concerned to control agriculture in order to feed their people and thus keep them from rebellion and to generate tax revenue. In the pre-unification state of Qin, measures were taken to prevent farmers from having access to timber and ponds where they might acquire wood or fish and turtles for free instead of concentrating on producing grain. Inspectors toured the country to make

神農氏因宜教田辟土種穀以振萬民

4. *The divine inventor of agriculture with a forked spade*

sure that agriculture was being conducted according to the best methods and to exhort the people 'to labour energetically'.[24]

The farmers working in the fields wore long- or short-sleeved knee-length tunics of coarse, beige undyed hemp cloth, over plain undergarments, with trousers or leggings underneath which they could roll up for work in the fields. They also wore rush or straw conical hats or the sort of stockinette caps seen on some of the soldiers in the First Emperor's Buried Army of terracotta warriors. If it rained, they put on coats made of coarse cloth or rushes. The characteristic indigo-dyed clothing worn by Chinese peasants in later periods does not seem to have been adopted until after the reign of the First Emperor, when regulations forbidding farmers from wearing dyed clothes were relaxed.[25] Ordinary women wore similar cross-over tunics with undergarments visible at the neck-line, but their tunics were longer, reaching to their ankles. The silk that was produced by the farmers, some of which would be woven by their wives and which produced a rich fertilizer from the silkworm droppings, was destined for the nobility, as a form of tax. The nobility wore long, loose, cross-over silk gowns reaching to the floor, with exaggeratedly long sleeves, silk underskirts, leggings and shoes.[26]

The reign of the First Emperor was the last in which purely local foods were consumed, for the expansion of the Han dynasty (206 BC–AD 220) towards the Central Asian desert and the Silk Road brought in many foodstuffs which are now staples in China but which were then introductions from the west. These included 'grapes, alfalfa, pomegranate, walnut, sesame, onion, caraway seeds, peas, coriander from Bactria and cucumber'.[27] In the lifetime of the First Emperor, the major grains were various types of millet and rice, mostly grown in the south but apparently also cultivated in the north, which

5. *Agricultural workers in short jackets and trousers*

was rather more humid than it is today.[28] Other vegetable foods (listed in the *Book of Poetry*, *c.* tenth to seventh century BC) include malva, melon, gourd, turnip, Chinese leek, lettuce, field sowthistle, common cattail, smartweeds, wild beans, lotus roots, mustard greens, garlic, spring onion, amaranth, water chestnuts, Chinese cabbage and bamboo shoots.[29] It also seems possible that peanuts, thought to be a New World plant, and broad beans may have been cultivated, along with more reliably attested soya beans.[30]

Meat came from domesticated dogs and pigs. Though mutton and beef seem generally to have been used chiefly for ritual offerings, they may have been eaten as well. Various types of wild deer, including the sika and the Père David deer, rabbits, wild dog, boar, wild horse, bear, badger, tiger, panther, several sorts of rat, monkeys and foxes were hunted and presumably used as food. Chickens were commonly consumed, as were 'goose, quail, partridge, pheasant, sparrow and curlew', and peacock and carp bones have been found in many archaeological sites, as have the remains of turtles and shellfish. Frogs, cicadas and snails may also have been eaten.[31]

Food was prepared by boiling, steaming, roasting, salting, pickling, drying and smoking, though not, apparently, stir-frying. It was flavoured with salt, sour plums, soy sauce, cinnamon, ginger and Sichuan pepper (fagara).[32] Cooking vessels were made of bronze or pottery, preserving jars of pottery, and food was served on pottery, plain wooden or lacquered wood dishes, with spoons, of wood or made from dried bottle gourds, and chopsticks. Spirits distilled from grain (this is before the arrival of grapes from the west) were drunk and used in ritual offerings.

Two of the *Songs of the South* of the early third century BC are calls to summon the soul of a dead ruler back to the land of the living, and

some of the most persuasive passages in them invoke feasts prepared
to welcome the soul home.

All kinds of good food are ready:
Rice ... early wheat, mixed all with yellow millet ...
Ribs of the fatted ox cooked tender and succulent;
Sour and bitter blended in the soup ...
Stewed turtle and roast kid, served up with yam sauce;
Geese cooked in sour sauce, casseroled duck, fried flesh of
    the great crane;
Braised chicken, seethed tortoise ...
Fried honey-cakes of rice flour and malt-sugar sweetmeats ...

Plump orioles, pigeons and geese, flavoured with broth of
    jackal's meat ...
Fresh turtle, succulent chicken, dressed with a sauce ...
Pickled pork, dog cooked in bitter herbs and zingiber-
    flavoured mince
And sour ... salad of artemisia ...
Fried bream, stewed magpies, and green goose, broiled.
Oh soul, come back! Choice things are spread before you.[33]

The lists convey the variety of cooking methods and mix of ingredients in the rich stews served at banquets. Guests would sit or kneel
on mats, for the chair did not come to China for another thousand
years, and perhaps lean on low stools for support. Dishes were placed
in strict order, with meat cooked on the bone to the left, sliced meats
to the right, grain on the left, soup on the right, together with
fermented drinks and spring onions and pickles beyond the dishes.[34]

6. *Bringing food to a banquet with dancing women in long silk gowns*

The food of ordinary farmers would of course have been infinitely simpler, with more grain (millet in the north, rice in the south) and vegetables and much less meat.

The farmers paid tax mainly in the form of grain and textiles, although there were some other commodities such as raw lacquer (produced from the sap of various trees) which could also be offered in payment. One of the major innovations of the First Emperor was to set up a national administration to collect taxes, replacing the previous Warring States system by which local rulers took the tax. The First Emperor's officials kept part of the tax for local use, maintained granaries for local relief and sent the rest to the capital.[35] Though many of the huge public works initiated by the First Emperor (canal-building, road-building, the Great Wall, his tomb and palaces) were carried out by convicts conscripted into labour service, farmers also owed labour and military service to the state.

The state of Qin in which the First Emperor grew up as the eldest son of the local ruler, was one which had already initiated great changes in the centralization of tax collection and agricultural control as well as in water management. The imposition of a strict series of laws, posted on stone pillars in front of the gates of the palace in the capital, was a third-century BC Qin innovation. The conquest of the other Warring States had also begun in the centuries before the First Emperor. He inherited ideas about centralized administration, law and legal responsibility and the need to standardize weights and measures but it was he who, through his conquest of the other states, was able to spread these ideas throughout the Chinese empire.

Some of the technological and engineering triumphs of this early period can still be seen today – the Great Wall, the First Emperor's tomb and Buried Army, the canal to the south and the Min River irrigation scheme. What did not survive the twentieth century but which endured for over 2,000 years was the Chinese bureaucracy, imposed by the First Emperor, the largest in the world, staffed by educated men and reaching to the lowest peasant in the land.

Despite these significant gifts to the Chinese empire, one of the most enduring aspects of the First Emperor's rule has been the reputation for appalling tyranny and cruelty that grew up around him.

I

The Heart of a Tiger or Wolf

Born in 259 BC, the son of the King of Qin and a concubine, the First Emperor was given the name Zheng, which means 'upright' or 'correct', although since he was born in the first month of the Chinese year, a month which bears the same name, he may have been named for the month as well as for the significance of the word.[1]

The state of Qin had, for over a century before his birth, been promoting new ideas of centralized bureaucracy (instead of the feudal rule of local aristocrats) and of law, with rules and regulations publicly posted on great pillars set up at the gates of the king's palace. Despite these progressive measures, Qin, on the western borders of the federation of Warring States that was then China, was regarded as 'barbarian', and has been ever since. Even in 1985, the great archaeologist and historian of early China, Li Xueqin, prefaced his account of the state of Qin by saying, 'The ancestors of the state of Qin were a tribe established by the Ying clan which lived among the Western Rong groups.' For Ying clan and Western Rong groups, read barbarians. Others would suggest that this ancestry was extremely distant and probably very mixed, particularly as a result of intermarriage and the mingling of cultures, and that it was largely as a result of later political interactions that the far north-west (where the state of Qin lay) became characterized as barbarian.[2]

On the death of his father in 247, when he was thirteen, Zheng became King of Qin, and his reign is traditionally described as beginning in 246 BC. Over the next two and a half decades, the armies of Qin defeated all the other Warring States and in 221 BC, the King of Qin took control of the whole of China and proclaimed himself the First Emperor. He died in 210 BC and the dynasty he had founded only outlasted him by four years.

Apart from this bare outline, the life of the First Emperor is difficult to trace without prejudice.[3] The main source is a history of China from the earliest beginnings to 100 BC, *The Grand Scribe's Records*, compiled by a court astrologer who died in about 85 BC, over a century after the First Emperor's death. The fall of a dynasty was traditionally regarded as being almost self-inflicted, corruption and weakness incurring the disapproval of Heaven and so bringing about the withdrawal of the Mandate of Heaven which legitimized 'good' rulers.[4] Inevitably, therefore, a new dynasty tended to be critical of the regime it had overthrown.

Writing as a court employee serving the Han dynasty, which had overthrown the Qin, the Grand Scribe would not have been expected to praise the First Emperor. His account, however, provides virtually all that is known about the man apart from stone inscriptions set up by the Emperor himself and the archaeological discoveries of his tomb and the remains of his palaces whose extent and elaboration fuelled traditional stories of excess and extravagance.

Blackening the name of the First Emperor began with stories about his birth. Before he became King of Qin in 249, the First Emperor's father was sent to another state as a hostage. This was a

7. *The First Emperor, depicted 1,500 years later*

recognized form of diplomacy at the time by which young princes were sent to rival states as a guarantee against attack. There, the young prince was befriended by a merchant who was later to become Prime Minister of Qin.[5] That his friend was described as a merchant was probably also a subtle slander: merchants were not held in high esteem in Chinese society, though in this early period they could achieve considerable power through their wealth.[6] The friend was not only a merchant but also, apparently, an ambitious schemer. On reportedly asking what sort of profit might be made from 'peddling pearls and jewellery', he was told a hundred per cent. 'How much then by helping a prince ascend the throne?' 'Why the profit would be infinite!'[7]

Thus, with the scheming merchant's encouragement, the young prince fell in love with one of the merchant's concubines and their son, born in 259 BC, was to become the First Emperor. However, it was alleged in *The Grand Scribe's Records* and elsewhere that the concubine was already pregnant and that the child was not the Prince's heir but the merchant's son.[8] Though this doubly slanderous passage is thought by scholars to have been a malicious insertion into the *Records*, it was nevertheless widely believed and added to the negative image of the First Emperor that persisted in China for over two thousand years.

The Prime Minister presided over the state when the First Emperor was young, while Qin armies were still waging war against neighbouring states, but he was accused in the *Records* of continuing to scheme with his ex-concubine, the mother of the First Emperor. Apparently not a jealous man, the Prime Minister introduced her to a famously well-hung gentleman who soon rebelled against the Qin. There is a complicated story associated with this rebel lover of the

First Emperor's mother. The Prime Minister is said to have had him condemned to castration but to have advised the Emperor's mother privately to have him pluck his eyebrows and beard. He would then appear to be a eunuch and so would be able to enter the women's quarters freely.[9] Whatever the truth of the story, the Prime Minister was condemned in 237 BC for his connection with the rebel and in 235 BC he committed suicide.

The Prime Minister may not have been loyal to the First Emperor, but his scholarly activities earned him the regard of future chroniclers. Concerned that the state of Qin did not value scholars as some of the other states did (an attitude that was to persist under the First Emperor), in 239 BC he organized a great gathering of scholars and encouraged them to write on 'all manner of things in heaven and on earth, past and present'. The result was named in his honour as *Master Lü's Spring and Autumn Annals*.[10] For succeeding dynasties, which officially revered scholarship, this was enough to erase, at least in part, his connection with the tyrannical First Emperor.

A year before the Prime Minister's disgrace, in 238 BC, as his armies continued to attack rival states, and after the appearance of a comet whose long tail stretched across the entire sky, the First Emperor was acknowledged as an adult in a ceremony in which he donned a cap and buckled on a sword.

The following year, the First Emperor received a visit from a man he was to make his Commandant. The *Records* include the only physical description of him by this visitor, who is supposed to have said, 'The King of Qin has a waspish nose, eyes like slits, a chicken breast and a voice like a jackal.' He continued with an equally damning description of his character: 'He is merciless, with the heart of a tiger or wolf.' Having been treated with apparent courtesy, sharing 'clothes, food and drink' with the First Emperor, the Commandant acknowledged his cunning: 'When in difficulties he willingly humbles himself, when successful he swallows men up without a scruple. I am a plain citizen in homespun clothes yet he treats me as if I were his superior. Should he succeed in conquering the [world], we shall all become his captives. There is no staying long with this man.'

This description was made by a man who had come to Qin with the express purpose of advising the First Emperor that, as well as waging war against rival states, he should consider bribery. 'For three thousand pieces of gold,' he suggested, Qin could 'conquer all the states'.[11]

Despite the continuing success of his armies, the First Emperor was not immune to danger. In 227, one of the northern states dispatched an assassin to make the first of three (unsuccessful) attempts on his life.[12] Not only did the First Emperor represent an increasingly alarming threat to rival states but he had also become known for his ruthless elimination of defeated armies. Even those who had surrendered on a promise of safety were often slaughtered regardless, and it was estimated that by 221 BC, over a million men, not counting Qin's own casualties, had been killed or taken prisoner.[13]

After a final push against the coastal state of Qi, the First Emperor was able to proclaim with rhetorical modesty, 'Insignificant as I am, I have raised troops to punish the rebellious princes; and thanks to the sacred power of our ancestors all six kings have been chastised as they deserved, so that at last the empire is pacified.'[14]

At this point, *The Grand Scribe's Records* offers a breathless summary of many of the major decisions and policies of the First Emperor: his choice of the title First Emperor as his designation, the adoption of a term equivalent to the 'royal we' to refer to himself in official proclamations, decisions on the symbolic cycle of the Five Elements (see below) and a proposal on how to control the massive empire without falling back into the disunion of the Warring States.[15]

The first decision, on his name, was one of enormous symbolic significance. He now ruled over a vast new territory and clearly wanted a title that went far beyond that of king. He declared himself Qin Shi huangdi. Qin was for his original state, 'Shi' means 'first', and 'huangdi' was a new compound with considerable religious and political significance. 'Huang' means 'august' or 'majestic' but the compound 'huangdi' was created to mean 'emperor'. The 'di' part of the compound was the most resonant. More than a thousand years earlier, the Shang rulers had worshipped 'di' as their supreme god. Several hundred years later, the legendary sages and rulers of antiquity, who were credited with the 'invention' of various fundamental activities such as agriculture, music and sericulture, were also elevated to the status of deities and named 'di'. An example is the legendary Yellow Emperor, 'Huangdi', who was said to have invented cooking and medicine.

The King of Qin was not the first mortal to consider the title of 'di', but his predecessors had failed in their attempts at self-elevation.[16] The successfully self-proclaimed First Emperor assumed a title that was retained by Chinese rulers until AD 1911. Moreover, it is probable that the state of Qin, which he ruled before the conquest and unification of the Warring States, provided the name by which China is still known throughout much of the world. Greek and Roman texts of the first and second centuries AD use the terms 'Thinai' and 'Sinai' respectively, and an Indian treatise of c. AD 150 uses the term 'Cina'.[17] The Chinese themselves never applied this name to their land. To them the whole empire was always known as the 'Middle or Central Kingdom' or Zhongguo, and the name persists to this day in Chinese.

After choosing his title, the First Emperor addressed the symbolism of the state according to the School of the Five Elements. The idea that five elements – earth, wood, metal, fire and water – each in turn dominated different periods of history was systematized in the third century BC. Each of the Five Elements had associated attributes of colour, cardinal direction and number. It was believed that the royal house of Zhou (1122–256 BC) had ruled through the power of fire[18]. Thus the new Qin dynasty must be ruled by water, the next element in the list. Red was the colour associated with fire and black the colour associated with water. The number associated with water was six. For the First Emperor 'black became the paramount colour for garments, flags and pennants, and six the paramount number. Tallies and official hats were six inches long, carriages six feet wide, one "pace" was six feet, and the imperial carriage had six horses.'[19] The dramatic picture of an imperial progress with its wide black chariots bearing black banners and flags, and carrying officials in their six-inch hats and black robes, passing farmers in neutrally coloured homespun jackets and trousers has been challenged by a spoilsport Japanese academic who thinks the whole passage was a later invention.[20]

One of the most significant innovations of Qin rule came after these decisions on symbols. This was a reversal of the system by which the Zhou had divided their realms, entrusting them to princes and nobles who had eventually set themselves up as kings, threatening the Zhou and creating the 'Warring States'. The First Emperor's

Councillor, Li Si, suggested that, since 'all lands within the Four Seas have become your provinces and counties', rather than 'setting up princes', the First Emperor should 'give the princes and men who served you well public revenues and rich rewards'. Abolishing the feudal system, for the purpose of administration, the Qin territory was divided into thirty-six provinces, 'each with a governor, an army commander and an inspector'.[21] The establishment of a civil administration, which was to be consolidated by succeeding dynasties, was one of the most significant contributions of the First Emperor to Chinese history.

To prevent further warfare, it was recorded that 'All the weapons were brought to the capital, where they were melted down to make bronze bells and twelve bronze statues of giants ... and these were placed in the courts and palaces. All weights and measures were standardized; all carriages had gauges of the same size. The script was also standardized.'[22]

In another move to prevent rebellion, the First Emperor insisted that the nobility move to his capital where he could keep an eye on them: 'One hundred and twenty thousand wealthy families were brought from all over the empire'[23] and forced to live in the capital at Xianyang, near present-day Xi'an, where massive construction work began on palaces, gardens and the imperial ancestral temple on the south bank of the Wei River. Nearby, musical instruments and beautiful women captured during the conquest were kept in specially constructed pavilions and courtyards.

The First Emperor also directed other massive moves of population. Some of these were of convicts, sent both north and south in 214 BC to subdue and colonize border areas, but others involved free families who were directed to colonize and farm underpopulated areas on the east coast in 219 BC, in return for twelve years' exemption from forced labour service.[24]

The forced colonization of the sparsely populated east coast was the result of one of the First Emperor's many tours of inspection or progresses through his new realms. These journeys were probably the result of a desire to familiarize himself with his massive empire and also to set his mark on it through the performance of ritual sacrifices at sacred spots and the erection of commemorative stelae on mountains. They were also another innovation of the First Emperor that became part of the imperial ritual in succeeding centuries. The most enthusiastic imperial travellers were the eighteenth-century Kangxi and Qianlong emperors whose progresses were recorded in elaborately detailed paintings.[25]

Mountains, long believed to be places where man and the gods could meet, became increasingly important later on in Chinese history, but when the First Emperor went to Mount Tai in Shandong province, there were arguments amongst the local scholars as to exactly what sort of ceremony should take place. For the mountain was regarded not just as a sacred place but as a sacred intermediary. Impatient with the dithering scholars, the First Emperor is said to have sacrificed in secret, before setting up a stone stele bearing an inscription proclaiming the greatness of his rule.[26] He also ennobled a tree under which he sheltered from a storm, making it a Minister of the Fifth Rank.[27] Though only parts of two of his stone inscriptions survive, the text of six is given in *The Grand Scribe's Records*. That from Mount Langya, on the coast in Shandong province, provides an account of the achievements of his reign, his policy of standardization, the imposition of the rule of law, the establishment of a civil administration and the initiation of great

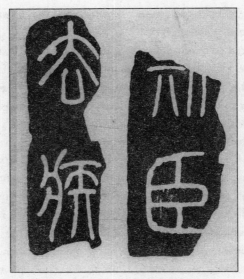

8. A Qin inscription in 'small seal' script

waterworks. It also sets out his view of the duties his citizens owe to him as a just ruler:

By the twenty-eighth year of his reign
A new age is inaugurated by the Emperor;
Rules and measures are rectified,
The myriad things set in order,
Human affairs are made clear.
And there is harmony between fathers and sons.
The Emperor in his sagacity, benevolence and justice
Has made all laws and principles manifest.
He set forth to pacify the east,

To inspect officers and men;
This great task accomplished
He visited the coast.
Great are the Emperor's achievements,
Men diligently attend to basic tasks,
Farming is encouraged, secondary pursuits discouraged,
All the common people prosper;
All men under the sky
Toil with a single purpose;
Tools and measures are made uniform,
The written script is standardized;
Wherever the sun and moon shine,
Wherever one can go by boat or by carriage,
Men carry out his orders
And satisfy their desires;
For our Emperor in accordance with the time
Has regulated local customs,
Made waterways and divided up the land.
Caring for the common people,
He works day and night without rest;
He defines the laws, leaving nothing in doubt,
Making known what is forbidden.
The local officials carry out their duties,
Administration is smoothly carried out,
All is done correctly, all according to plan,
The Emperor in his wisdom
Inspects all four quarters of his realm;
High and low, noble and humble,
None dare overshoot the mark;

No evil or impropriety is allowed,
All strive to be good men and true,
And exert themselves in tasks great and small;
None dares to idle or ignore his duties,
But in far-off remote places
Serious and decorous administrators
Work steadily, just and loyal.
Great is the virtue of our Emperor
Who pacifies all four corners of the earth,
Who punishes traitors, roots out evil men,
And with profitable measures brings prosperity.
Tasks are done at the proper season,
All things flourish and grow;
The common people know peace
And have laid aside weapons and armour;
Kinsmen care for each other,
There are no robbers or thieves;
Men delight in his rule,
All understanding the law and discipline.
The universe entire is our Emperor's realm ...
Wherever human life is found,
All acknowledge his suzerainty,
His achievements surpass those of the Five Emperors,
His kindness reaches even the beasts of the field;
All creatures benefit from his virtue,
All live in peace at home.[28]

Setting up such inscriptions recording his benevolence took place every time he ascended a significant mountain. In the thirtieth year of his reign (216 BC), 'nothing of moment occurred', but in the next year he is recorded as walking through the capital dressed as a commoner and being set upon by bandits who were beaten off by his bodyguards. In 215 BC, he ordered General Meng north with 300,000 men and in 213 he decreed that all legal officials who had failed to deliver justice should go north to build the Great Wall or be exiled to the south. In the same year, perhaps under pressure from his Councillor, he ordered the destruction of all books excluding those on divination, medicine and agriculture, one of the most criticized actions of his rule. He attracted further criticism for embarking on massive building projects near the capital, creating a grandiose palace and gardens and beginning work on his extravagant tomb nearby.

As he approached middle age, the First Emperor became increasingly interested in the pursuit of immortality and susceptible to charlatans. He also became increasingly secretive and suspicious. His eldest son, who dared to criticize him, was sent off to join General Meng on the northern frontier. In 219 he had sent an expedition, including several thousand young boys and girls, to search for the fabled Island of the Immortals, supposed to be off the eastern coast of China. The expedition never returned, and in 215 he sent another, this time consisting of only three men, to search for the island and for the herbs and drugs conferring immortality that would surely be found there. He was informed that they failed to reach the island because they were frightened by an enormous fish. In 210, when he set off again on his travels, taking one of his youngest sons with him, he sailed down the Yangtze and then up the eastern coast, in search of the giant fish. He spent some time on the shore, waiting with a repeating crossbow, and eventually shot a large fish. But when he turned inland, he fell ill. Before he died, he managed to write a message, impressed with the imperial seal, to his eldest son, still in the far north with General Meng. It was clear that the First Emperor intended that his eldest son should succeed him, but his Councillor had other ideas.

The First Emperor's corpse decomposed rapidly. To disguise the smell, a cart of rotting fish accompanied the imperial carriage on the long journey back to the capital. There, the Councillor forged a letter for the First Emperor's eldest son, accusing him of being unfilial and ordering him to commit suicide, which he did. The same order was given to General Meng who, however, refused to succumb until 207 when he took poison. The First Emperor was succeeded by the son who had travelled with him on his last journey. So little is known about the family life of the First Emperor that we do not know if the Second Emperor was his youngest son or number eighteen out of about twenty sons.[29]

2

The Grand Scribe's Records and the Place of the Sleeping Tiger

For two thousand years, *The Grand Scribe's Records*, compiled on the basis of texts surviving in the Han imperial library, was the only major source of information on the life and reign of the First Emperor.[1] But in 1975, at the Place of the Sleeping Tiger, about seventy-five kilometres north-west of Wuhan in Hubei province, excavation of the tomb of a Qin dynasty official who had died in 217 BC at the age of forty-five, revealed a cache of documents.[2] Preserved in the waterlogged tomb, the documents included sections of the Qin legal code that the official needed to consult in his administrative duties, a question-and-answer book explaining the legal terms used by officials, and a book of divination. The texts were written on long, narrow strips of bamboo which were tied together and rolled up for storage. Though paper was probably invented at about this time in China, it took some centuries before it became widely used. All early books and texts in central and southern China were written on such narrow strips of bamboo, and in the north on narrow strips of wood.[3]

The importance of the legal texts is enormous for they reveal that, contrary to the traditional view that the First Emperor used law as a cruel and arbitrary weapon against his people, the laws and punishments were in fact clearly set out and carefully graded, with differing circumstances taken into account (see Chapter 5).

The divination text, rather than recommending consultation of the gods or the throwing of stalks of yarrow, as in the *Book of Changes*, listed auspicious days for particular activities, as traditional Chinese almanacs do to this day. There were good days and bad days for arresting criminals or trying them, lucky days and unlucky days for marrying, holding a funeral or building a wall. There was also advice on subjects such as marriage (marriage to a talkative or ugly or sickly and infertile wife was discouraged).[4] Though this document tells us much about the daily life of the Qin and may inform us on decisions made by the First Emperor, it tells us nothing about his life. For that we have to fall back on *The Grand Scribe's Records*.

Written in a clear yet elegant style, the *Records* is one of the most influential works in Chinese historiography, setting a style that was to be followed for over a thousand years as each new dynasty in China wrote up the history of its predecessor.[5] As has already been noted, the approach was often critical, the fall of a dynasty being regarded as the result of corruption and weakness that prompted the withdrawal of the Mandate of Heaven.[6]

Though Sima Qian is usually assumed to have been the main author of the *Records*, he gives much credit to his father, Sima Tan (d. 108 BC), whom he succeeded as Prefect of the Grand Scribes, a job that involved 'the supervision of sacrifices and the calendar, the management of astrological questions, and the care of the imperial library'.[7] His father seems to have begun the ambitious task of

9. The Grand Scribe

writing down all of China's history from its very beginning, since he regarded it as a filial duty (his ancestors had all been Grand Scribes). He was also distressed at the failure of the Han imperial house to emulate the enlightened rulers of the past, whose deeds he wanted to set down. The idea that a historical record would highlight the ethical rulers of the past and castigate 'bad' rulers produced a form of stereotyping that became characteristic of much Chinese historical writing, and it was the fate of the First Emperor to be stereotyped as a 'bad' ruler.[8]

In order to continue his father's historical work, the second Grand Scribe would have worked in the imperial library from historical texts written on narrow strips of bamboo or wood, though he may also have used inscriptions from bronzes cast in the early (or Western) Zhou period (1045–771 BC) in particular, which recorded wars, kingly favours and gifts of land, and possibly stone inscriptions.[9]

The documents from the Place of the Sleeping Tiger are original Qin documents, but so far no early copies of *The Grand Scribe's Records* have been unearthed. The story of the work is further complicated by the attitude of his employer to the Grand Scribe himself. Perhaps imbued by the ideas of 'goodness' and loyalty that were to characterize his work, the Grand Scribe made the mistake of defending an army commander who had been betrayed whilst fighting bravely against the Xiongnu barbarians in the north. For this unpopular view, he was sentenced either to death or to castration. He chose the latter in order to be able to continue his father's work before he died in about 86 BC. Though he was later rehabilitated through a descendant who, sometime between AD 9 and 23, was given the title 'The Viscount Who Comprehends History', the survival of his *Records* is a complex story.

Subsequent historians working in the later Han dynasty (in the first century AD) seem to have had access to the text through the imperial library and, indeed, incorporated many passages from it in their own histories, but the text itself has only survived through later copies. The earliest surviving editions date from the Song dynasty (960–1279), considerably after the original compilation.[10]

Scholars agree that the text as known today includes many insertions of passages and texts by other authors. Some of these may have been made quite early on, such as an essay by a poet and statesman (Jia Yi, 201–169 BC) entitled 'The Faults of Qin'.[11] This summarized the First Emperor's achievements in negative terms:

Cracking his long whip, he drove the universe before him ...

overthrowing the feudal lords. He ascended to the highest position and ruled the six directions, scourging the world with his rod, and his might shook the four seas ... In the south he seized the land ... and the hundred lords bowed their heads, hung halters from their necks, and pleaded for their lives ... Then he caused General Meng to build the Great Wall and defend the borders ... so that the barbarians no longer dared to come south to pasture their horses and their men dared not take up arms to avenge their hatred. Thereupon he discarded the ways of the former kings and burned the writings of the hundred schools in order to make the people ignorant ... He collected all the arms of the empire and had them brought to his capital ... where the spears and arrowheads were melted down ... He garrisoned the strategic points with skilled generals and expert bowmen and stationed trusted ministers and well-trained soldiers to guard the land with arms and questioned all who passed back and forth.[12]

No mention is made in this text of the achievements of the First Emperor which were recorded in the stone inscriptions he set up on his visits to major mountains across China. In the texts of those that do survive,[13] instead of stressing military control, the First Emperor describes his efforts to control his empire through standardization and through the rule of law and the encouragement of agriculture, traits that have not made their way into the historical tradition.

3

The Cunning Councillor

The burning of the books was suggested to the First Emperor by his Councillor in 213 BC and, though the traditional view is that it was the First Emperor who was responsible for this and other barbarities during his reign, some consider the Councillor to have been the power behind the imperial throne.

Born some time around 280 BC, the Councillor came from a state in the far south.[1] According to his biography in *The Grand Scribe's Records*, he considered the local ruler unworthy of his service. He reached a similar conclusion regarding the rulers of the other Warring States and decided to 'go westward to give counsel to the King of Qin'.[2] He managed to enter the household of the Prime Minister and was eventually appointed 'Alien Minister', a title given to advisors who came from outside Qin. Ironically, one of his first challenges in the post was to consider the expulsion of all aliens which would, of course, have included himself. The expulsion had been proposed in 237 BC by members of the King's family, who had been alarmed by a complex plot organized by an 'alien', which involved the construction of a canal. According to *The Grand Scribe's Records*, the proposal to build the canal, which would be 300 li (approximately 160 kilometres) long and irrigate a substantial area, was intended to draw large numbers of men into construction work and away from army service, thus reducing the threat to neighbouring states. The only problem with this story is that other sources put the construction of the canal in 246 BC, some ten years before the proposal to expel aliens was made.

Whatever the provocation, the proposal was opposed by the Councillor in a long and eloquent speech. He pointed out that the palace was filled with women from other states that were famous for the beauty of their women, and that the First Emperor hung beautiful pearls from distant parts on his belt and treasured jade from the far-off Kunlun mountains. He rode imported horses and his drummers beat their rhythms on imported crocodile-skin drums. Without imports, there would be no cinnabar or lapis to adorn the painted palace and 'no utensils of rhinoceros horn or ivory'. The proposal to expel immigrants, whilst at the same time allowing the import of beautiful women and exotic materials, seemed to imply that human beings were not valued. He also suggested that the expulsion of alien advisors would have the effect of strengthening the other states: 'this is what is known as offering weapons to brigands and presenting provisions to robbers'.[3] This elegant speech convinced the First Emperor that he should revoke the order.

Though his patron the Prime Minister was disgraced in the same year (237 BC) and committed suicide two years later, the Councillor's own performance at court made his position secure and he is associated with most of the major reforms of the First Emperor. According to *The Grand Scribe's Records*, when the First Emperor's advisors recommended setting up members of the imperial family to rule over remote regions, assuming them to be loyal, it was the

Councillor who proposed the abolition of the old feudal system which had, in the past, led to dissension and war, and its replacement with a government based on commanderies or provinces, each with a civil administrator, a general and an inspector.

Similarly, according to the *Records*, in 213 BC, when the First Emperor was challenged by scholars for his radical reforms which broke with tradition, it was the Councillor who proposed that in order to prevent dissent through endless harking back to the supposed glories of the past, books containing such information be destroyed, leaving only useful, practical manuals on agriculture and medicine. The First Emperor adopted his Councillor's proposal.

Looking at *The Grand Scribe's Records*, it is interesting to see that the Councillor leads these initiatives while the bulk of the entries referring to the First Emperor's own activities after 221 BC describe his lengthy trips of inspection to the far corners of his realm and the great stone stelae he set up recording his achievements. His growing interest in the search for physical (and consequently spiritual) immortality is evident, as is his interest in portents and divination. The balance of the *Records* shows the Councillor as statesman and the First Emperor as increasingly distanced from daily affairs of state.[4]

The Councillor's involvement in the schemes that followed the First Emperor's death show him in a very different light, however. He was travelling with the First Emperor in 210 BC when the Emperor died, hundreds of miles from the capital. The death of the Emperor and the absence of the Councillor from the capital created a dangerous power vacuum, the more so since the official heir, the First Emperor's eldest son, was also far away. He had been sent north with General Meng as a form of exile for having 'several times frankly remonstrated' with his father. On his last journey, the

9. A covered chariot

First Emperor had taken a younger son along with him. Before he died, and knowing that he was fatally ill, he had dictated a letter to his eldest son, asking him to bring General Meng's soldiers to accompany the funeral cortege to the capital, where he was to be buried. It is possible that the impracticability of summoning the heir from his distant exile played a part in the Councillor's subsequent decisions.

The First Emperor had died in midsummer. The Councillor decided to take his body back to the capital but to conceal the fact of his death. It was said that the Emperor 'was keeping to his sleeping chariot. The various officials continued to submit their affairs and [a pretence was kept up that] the Emperor ate food as before. The eunuchs who ... accompanied the sleeping chariot [pretended to transmit the royal] approval on the affairs that were submitted.'[5] Despite the pretence, the imperial body was decaying rapidly and

43

the Councillor ordered that a cart loaded with salted fish, decaying at the same rate, follow the procession.[6]

The First Emperor's letter to his eldest son was not sent. Instead, the Chief Eunuch (a man reported as confidently describing 'a deer as a horse'[7]) conspired with the First Emperor's younger son to convince the Councillor that, should the eldest son succeed, he would certainly choose General Meng as his chief advisor and the Councillor would be forced to return to his village. Eventually they composed a letter in the name of the First Emperor accusing his heir of being unfilial and presenting him with a sword with which he was ordered to kill himself. General Meng was also ordered to commit suicide and, despite his protests, eventually followed the example of the First Emperor's heir, though not before declaring that his only crime was an infraction of *feng shui* – he had cut through mountains when building the Great Wall.[8] The First Emperor's eighteenth or twentieth son (the *Records* are unclear on the matter) was proclaimed as Second Emperor in 210 BC, but his reign was short-lived. Rebellions broke out immediately and he was overthrown and killed in 207 BC. (It is interesting to note that despite his reputation for savagery, no popular uprisings were reported during the reign of the First Emperor.)

As an advisor to the Second Emperor, the Councillor is said to have resorted to the strategy he had earlier despised. In criticizing the Second Emperor, he accused him of ignoring the lessons of the past in giving himself up to women and music. For this, the Councillor was condemned to death by being cut in half in the market place in the capital in 208 BC. According to *The Grand Scribe's Records*, before the sentence was carried out, he made a further long accusation against the Second Emperor, accusing him of overspending on palace building, overtaxing his people and slaying his other brothers.[9]

Under the First Emperor, whose major undertaki[ng]
to have originated in the Councillor's decisions, the Cou[n]
held a position of ultimate power. Under the son he found hi[m]
excluded from the inner court and so unable to influence policy. His
failure to establish himself in the same position of trust with the
Second Emperor may have resulted partly from his dubious activities in disobeying his former master's orders and not appointing
the rightful heir. He may also have been outmanoeuvred by the
Chief Eunuch, for whom court intrigue was more important than
statesmanship.

Cowboys and Indians or Confucianism and Legalism

In 1964, Arthur Waley published a book called *Three Ways of Thought in Ancient China*, which for the first time introduced a Western audience to the ideas of Confucianism, Daoism and what he termed 'realist' thought through translations of passages from significant texts.[1]

The revival of interest in the First Emperor and his policies during the Cultural Revolution (1966–76) presented an even simpler picture of the philosophy of the period, dividing all thinkers and scholars into just two groups, the followers of Confucianism (bad) and of Legalism (good). In this division, Confucius (551–479 BC), whose ideas became fundamental to the state throughout Chinese imperial history, was a reactionary, always looking back to the legendary past, preoccupied only with propping up the ruler through mumbo-jumbo rituals and unconcerned about the fate of the suffering peasants. The Legalists were good because they set up an administration run by men of talent, promoted economic growth through the encouragement of agriculture, standardization and improvements in communications, and set out clear laws by which all lived. The Legalists were practical, the Confucians impractical. Unfortunately the picture of Chinese thought in the Warring States and Qin periods is much more complicated than that.

As with the historical records, one of the great problems is that of sources. There are no books as such, written by a single author, surviving from before the Qin. As one scholar puts it, such 'books' as we have, 'no matter whose names they bear, are obviously layered texts that "grew" over the centuries or are suspected to have been added to, or taken from, rearranged, or pieced together after the main author (if there was one) died'.[2]

Confucius was traditionally associated with the Five Classics, two of which were specifically recommended for burning by the First Emperor and his Councillor. The *Book of Poetry*, proscribed by the First Emperor, contained 305 songs, traditionally supposed to have been composed around 1000 BC, though many date from several centuries later and, despite the legend that Confucius himself gathered them together, have nothing to do with him except that they were known to him.[3] The other text now described as one of the Five Classics and singled out by the First Emperor and his Councillor for destruction was a historical work, the *Book of Documents*. Though purporting to date from the third millennium BC to the seventh century BC, only a tiny proportion of it may be that early: it seems likely that the text was partly destroyed and then largely 'reconstituted' in the third or fourth century AD, so the connections with Confucius are tenuous, if they exist at all.[4]

Another of the Five Classics, associated with Confucius but not condemned by the First Emperor (he spared works on divination), is the *Book of Changes*, probably compiled in the ninth century BC, long before Confucius. This set out a method of divination using yarrow or milfoil stalks, which were to be interpreted by means of eight trigrams, 'permutations of three-line combinations of complete or broken lines', or, when six lines were used, sixty-four hexagrams.[5] Though foretelling the outcome of actions and predicting natural phenomena by means of heating ox shoulder bones or turtle shells had been practised by the Shang kings in the second millennium BC, the *Book of Changes* allowed a far wider use of divination.

Even the text which provides most information about Confucius himself, the *Judgements and Conversations*, apparently recording his conversations with his disciples and usually translated as the *Analects of Confucius*, was certainly written after his death, the latest passages added in about 250 BC.[6] It records incidents in his life such as the time he refused to see a Minister whom he considered an unworthy character. The Minister sent him a pig, knowing that a man so concerned with propriety and good manners would be compelled to thank him for it. However, the cunning philosopher chose a time when he knew the Minister was not at home to go and deliver his thanks.[7] Confucius emerges as a somewhat obsessional character, unable to sit comfortably if his mat wasn't straight, insisting on a nightshirt twice as long as himself and refusing to talk at meals.[8] When he did speak, he is reported as saying of himself, 'I set my heart on the Way, base myself on virtue, lean upon benevolence for support and take my recreation in the arts.'

It is perhaps easier to describe the philosophical and political theories of the period up to and including the First Emperor's reign by looking at preoccupations rather than individual theorists, many of whose ideas have reached us through many hands.

With the breakdown of centralized rule that culminated in the

10. Confucius discussing ritual in a temple

Warring States period (475–221 BC), war between separate states became endemic. It was only natural, therefore, that men had a tendency to look back to a time before such conflict and to idealize it, hence the significance of texts such as the *Book of Documents* which purported to relate ancient history. Even in troubled times, family relationships remained important, and family obligations, particularly the virtue of filiality or obedience towards and respect for parents and ancestors, were expressed through attention to ritual. Ritual was also important outside the family circle for it was seen as a means of keeping social order (Confucius emphasized that such

49

ritual should not be empty but rather should always be meaningful and sincere).

The good man or the good ruler was described as having moral force (more often translated as 'virtue', though the word has rather different connotations for us now). Such virtue was the result of self-cultivation by an individual. The relationship between master and disciple or ruler and advisor should also cultivate virtue, one aspect of which was seen as being able to listen and therefore understand. Benevolence (which Confucius stressed) was another aspect of the desired character of the 'gentleman', as opposed to the 'small man' who could hardly hope to aspire to that state. An extension of benevolence was the rather more down-to-earth doctrine of consideration for others: 'Do not impose on others what you yourself do not desire.'[9]

A subject that Confucius discussed and which was to be much debated, by 'legalist' thinkers as well as Confucians, was 'the rectification of names'. His most famous pronouncement on the subject was his prescription for stability in society: 'Let the ruler be a ruler, the subject a subject, the father a father and the son a son.'[10] Behind that simple sentence, stating that each man should know his place, was the implicit understanding that the appropriate rituals would be correctly performed and 'virtue' maintained. However, on another occasion he went further, explaining that, should he ever rule a state, the first thing he would do would be to 'rectify the names', otherwise everything would fall apart. 'When names are not correct, what is said will not sound reasonable; when what is said does not sound reasonable, affairs will not culminate in success; when affairs do not culminate in success, rites and music will not flourish; when rites and music do not flourish, punishments will not fit the crimes.'[11] Confu-

cius referred only to government and society, though later philosophers extended the idea of meaning into conundrums. 'The eye does
not see' (because it is you who see) and, most famously, 'a white
horse is not a horse'. Gongsun Long (b. *c.* 308 BC) explained that
you could say that a white horse was not a horse because ' "horse" is
that by which we name the shape, "white" is that by which we name
the colour. To name the colour is not to name the shape. Therefore I
say a white horse is not a horse.'[12] The white horse conundrum may
antedate this conversation because one of the great proponents of
Confucianism, Mencius (*c.* 372–289 BC) discussed the question of
whether a white horse's 'white' was like an old man's 'white', a sign
of age and hence deserving of respect.[13]

Mencius developed Confucius' basic tenets, particularly stressing
the idea that heaven-endowed human nature has a propensity to
good, exemplified in shared human values such as a love of fine
music, beauty and fine food, though self-cultivation is still necessary to achieve the Confucian ideals of benevolence, dutifulness,
propriety or attention to ritual, and moral intelligence.[14] His view
of the original goodness of man was directly contradicted by Xunzi
(*c.* 310–*c.* 210 BC) who thought men could only be brought into line
by continuous education. Mencius also wrote of the duty of a ruler to
order agriculture and bemoaned the uncontrolled deforestation that
he saw taking place.[15]

Another school of thought, that of the Taoists or Daoists, today
often associated with nature and natural harmony, was in the third
century BC not yet constituted as a 'school' or group but consisted
of a number of teachers who practised 'breathing techniques, meditation or austere eating regimes in the hope of extending [their]
lifespan or even of gaining immortality'.[16]

The two major texts associated with Daoism 'grew' like the Confucian texts.

The Way and Integrity, or *Daodejing* (third century BC), seems to have been a multi-author collection on the essentially indefinable *dao* or 'way', 'mystery of all mysteries'.[17] Based in part on older ideas such as the division of all in nature into *yin* and *yang*, it advocates non-action or non-interference, in other words a belief in letting things follow their natural course. Rulers should emulate water or a woman who, though weak, 'always conquers the male through her stillness'. Daoism esteems items untouched by human effort, such as raw silk and 'unhewn logs', and suggests, contrary to the Confucian stress on education, that if learning is abolished, 'you will be without worries'.[18]

The second Daoist classic is associated with Zhuangzi (*c.* 355–275 BC) and, like the Confucian *Judgements and Conversations*, consists largely of anecdotes, mostly of a paradoxical nature. When Zhuangzi dreamed he was a butterfly, was it him dreaming of being a butterfly or a butterfly dreaming of being Zhuangzi? When his wife died, instead of affecting public grief, he was found drumming cheerfully on a basin. He explained that his wife was merely sleeping in the Great Inner Room and thus he accepted nature's course.

These paradoxical puzzles and the lofty idealism of Confucius held little appeal for practical thinkers who wanted to find concrete methods of improving government and the livelihood of the people. Xunzi, who disagreed with Mencius over basic human nature, visited the state of Qin in about 258 BC, not long before the First Emperor took control, and commented upon the Legalist policies which were already being practised there. Though he believed in control, he thought that the Qin terrorized their people with their authority,

11. *A Daoist recluse contemplating the imponderable*

coaxed them with rewards and cowed them with punishments.[19] Whatever the views of the philosopher, the tight control exercised by the Qin rulers was soon to bring them ultimate power, as they triumphed over all neighbouring states.

Lord Shang, Prime Minister in Qin in the fourth century BC, regarded many Confucian virtues as parasitical and inimical to the military and agricultural success of the state. He described the 'six [actually seven] parasites' (enumerating them in pairs, so that there are in fact fourteen) as 'rites and music, odes and history, moral culture and virtue, filial piety and brotherly love, sincerity and faith, benevolence and righteousness, criticism of the army and being ashamed of fighting'.[20] Thus the benevolence which Confucius stressed, the ritual by which he set so much store and the odes and history which he venerated but which would later be outlawed by the First Emperor, were all condemned as weaknesses that would lay a state open to defeat.

Lord Shang may have initiated a scheme by which farmers, instead of working on the estates of noblemen, worked their own land. They were registered and grouped into small settlements, each comprising eight families. The eight family groups 'protected one another ... they took turns in keeping watch, in sickness they condoled with each other, in distress they assisted one another, those who had lent to those who had not, on festive occasions they invited each other, they arranged marriages for each other, they shared the results of fishing and hunting with each other'.[21] There was a drawback to this system, however. The eight families were responsible for each other to the extent that they could all be punished for one person's crime and thus there was a tendency to spy on and to betray one another for self-protection.[22]

Lord Shang believed that only agriculture and the army mattered to the state. Merchants and scholars could look after themselves but it was agriculture that produced the surplus grain that supported the army, and it was the army that made the state strong and overcame enemies. He had some practical advice to give on civil defence when attacked. Able-bodied men should be mustered with weapons to defend the city whilst all the able-bodied women should stand behind, ready to raise earthworks, dig pits for the enemy to fall into and pull down houses. All the old men in turn should be set to tend the animals and gather food and water to supply the able-bodied men and women. It was important, however, to keep these three groups apart, in case the fighting men were distracted from their task.[23]

At all times, the people were to be kept in check by laws, punishments and rewards, and it is clear that Lord Shang felt these should be clear, strict and strictly administered: there was no room for benevolence. He also advised that 'If the penalties are heavy and rewards few, then the ruler loves his people and they will die for you; if rewards are heavy and penalties light, the ruler does not love his people nor will they die for him.'[24] An example of how this reward system worked was in the army where soldiers gained promotion through the number of severed heads they submitted: the more heads they acquired, the higher their status.[25] It is worth noting that in China, the law was not considered to have been handed down from God as in the Judaic tradition, nor was it particularly associated with philosophers as in Greece: it was very much a practical tool, developed for practical reasons.[26]

Though the philosopher Xunzi may have criticized the laws of Qin as too harsh when he visited, the Councillor who was so closely associated with the First Emperor had been one of his students, and it was the Councillor who was responsible for many of the Legalist policies of the First Emperor's reign. The rejection of Confucian benevolence and ritual and their replacement with Legalism did not long survive the First Emperor's death. In the succeeding Han dynasty, Confucianism was established as the state ideology and remained as such throughout China's imperial history. Even so, many of Legalism's fundamental ideas persisted for just as long, in particular the need for a legal system to underpin the state and the idea of family grouping and mutual responsibility.

5

The Height of Legal
Responsibility

'The cruel laws of the cruel state of Qin are a byword in traditional
Chinese historiography,' wrote Professor Hulsewe in the introduction to a work which revealed how (relatively) unfounded this
byword was.[1] The earliest surviving Chinese legal code is that of
AD 635, preserved in a revised version made in 725. Earlier legal
codes can to some extent be reconstructed from other sources: literature, inscriptions and the Chinese histories in which each succeeding
dynasty recorded the history of the dynasty it had just overthrown.
These histories include quotations from official documents and some
also contain sections on the law, recording revisions and codifica-
tions. Though the Han dynasty, which overthrew the Qin in 206
BC, is said to have based its own legal code on that of the Qin, this
did not prevent traditional historians from viewing the Qin code as
cruel and that of the Han as relatively civilized.

Passages from the Qin code, datable to 217 BC, and a legal hand-
book found amongst the documents unearthed at the Place of the
Sleeping Tiger in 1975 have for the first time enabled us to judge

how harsh the laws of Qin were. The tomb was that of an official dealing with various aspects of the law, and the texts were written with brush and ink on narrow bamboo slips. Out of 1,200 bamboo slips originally placed inside the coffin, about 1,155 have survived and most have been transcribed. This was no easy task, for the strings joining the bamboo slips which kept them in order had decayed so that their original order had to be reconstructed.

Apart from a couple of texts on divination, listing auspicious and inauspicious days for various activities, a previously unknown history of the Qin and a collection of military edicts dating to 227 BC, the most important text fragments are those dealing with the law. Whether this was so that the dead official could continue to transact legal business in the spirit world or whether he was so attached to the tools of his trade that they were buried with him, we do not know.

Two hundred and one of the bamboo slips record regulations from the Qin legal code. The regulations deal with official tasks ranging from agricultural supervision to feeding and clothing those on labour service. These slips were placed on the right side of the body together with sixty slips recording regulations relating to accounting and unifying systems of measurement. Beside these there was also a series of slips relating to military affairs in legal terms. The most fascinating text is 'Questions and Answers on the Law', not strictly part of the legal code but a collection of case law, found by the neck of the dead man.[2]

The statutes or regulations were written on regular strips 27 centimetres long with an average of 35 characters on those that were fully inscribed. The statutes emphasize the importance of agriculture to the state which needed to build up full granaries in order to feed the army. There were recommendations and prohibitions on certain activities at certain times. Dogs should not be taken out hunting 'in the season of young animals' and if commoners allowed their dogs to kill animals in 'forbidden parks' they were to be killed and their pelts handed over to the government. Officials were required to make frequent reports in writing on the state of local agriculture, reporting on the number of fields with a good grain crop and also on 'drought and violent wind or rain, floods, hordes of grasshoppers or other creatures which damage the crops'.[3] The official reports were to be sent by runner if the official lived near the capital, or by the official courier service if he lived further away: another statute provided instructions on how to feed horses used by the official courier service, before they set off and when they returned, with extra rations permitted in the case of particularly hard work.

Care of animals that were the property of the government must have been a worrying task, for the animals had to be counted, measured and inspected four times a year. If they were in good condition at the major inspection in the first month of the administrative year (which during the Qin was the equivalent of November[4]), the Overseer of Agriculture was rewarded with 'a bottle of wine and a bundle of dried meat'. If the cattle were found to have lost weight, the person in charge was 'bastinadoed with ten strokes for each inch' of girth lost.[5] If three or more oxen (out of a set of ten) died within a year, everyone was deemed guilty, from the officials in charge down to those who fed the animals, although their punishment is not stipulated.

The government granaries were filled with grain according to sets of detailed instructions. The grain was to be stored in piles of 10,000 bushels, carefully weighed in the presence of several officials.

12. Supervisory officials and government horses and chariots

When the granary was full, it was to be sealed, again in the presence of several witnesses, and if rain subsequently got in, the official in charge was punished. Though the details do not appear in these official statutes, in 'Questions and Answers on the Law' found in the same tomb, the response to the query, 'How many rat holes in a granary warrant sentencing or berating?' is 'It is the practice of the court that for three or more rat holes, the fine is a shield and that for two or less the responsible official is berated. Three mouse holes are equivalent to one rat hole.'[6]

It is not known quite what 'berating' meant. The official might have had a public dressing-down, or perhaps a bamboo slip recording his misdemeanour was placed in his file. Fines paid by officials frequently took the form of a shield (worth 1,000 cash) or, more seriously, a suit of armour or several suits of armour. Local officials were also responsible for the care and maintenance of government-owned arms and armour. Each piece of military equipment had to be clearly marked with the name of the government agency which held it, either incised or painted in vermilion or lacquer. The same was true of agricultural tools owned by the government. And when arms or armour were loaned out, presumably in times of war, they had to be checked on return: if they were unmarked or bore the mark of another government agency, they were confiscated. This confiscation by the government of government property is rather mystifying, but it is possible that the official concerned would have had to make up the deficit.[7]

Much of the concern of a local official lay in the control of those who were working on government projects: building walls, making roads, constructing irrigation schemes or, in the case of women, pounding grain. Some of these were conscripted, others were criminals sentenced to hard labour, normally for a period of three years. During the Qin, boys were liable to conscription at the age of fifteen and served for two years, either in the army or on labour service. Care was taken not to remove more than one adult male from a household at any one time so that a family's normal way of life could be maintained.

The amount of food and number of meals supplied to these labourers was carefully listed, and extra rations were permitted for those working on heavy tasks. The normal ration was two bushels of grain per month for men and one and half bushels per month for women and 'small' people, with the ration raised to two and a half bushels (for men) in the busy agricultural season.[8] They were also issued with clothing.

> Summer clothing will be issued from the fourth until the end of the sixth month; winter clothing will be issued from the ninth till the end of the tenth month. No issues are to be made beyond these times ... For convicts who suffer from the cold, clothes of coarse hemp are to be made. To make one head-cloth, use three catties of hemp ... for one large jacket eighteen catties of hemp ... for one medium jacket fourteen catties of hemp ... for a small jacket use eleven catties of hemp; value 36 cash.

Whether a catty then weighed the same as a catty today seems unlikely. If it did, a large convict who suffered from the cold would be wearing three-quarters of a kilo of cloth on his head and staggering around in a jacket weighing four and a half kilos.[9]

One of the most interesting revelations of the Qin code is that, instead of the concept of an age of legal responsibility, it preferred to judge responsibility by height, a concept that was to persist, for it also occurs in the Tang code of AD 725. (As recently as 1975–6, in Beijing, buses had a metre-high mark at the entrance: children under one metre travelled free.[10]) This simple system, by which those under a metre and a half were considered too young to suffer adult punishment, could cause problems when a miscreant suddenly shot up between the time the crime was committed and the time he was brought to justice. Help for a puzzled magistrate was at hand, for 'Questions and Answers on the Law' offers a precedent. 'A. steals an ox; at the time he stole the ox he was six feet tall [the Qin foot was smaller than today's imperial measurement]. Having been held in detention for one year, he was measured again; he was six feet seven inches. Question: how is A. to be sentenced? He warrants being made into an intact "wall-builder".'[11] The sentence is one of hard labour but without the additional punishment of mutilation, in this case tattooing. In other words, he is sentenced less harshly than if he had been of adult height at the time he stole the ox.

Other cases listed in the 'Questions and Answers on the Law' include the case of the theft of a goat which happened to have a rope round its neck worth one copper coin. The magistrate was advised not to add the value of the rope to that of the goat since the goat was what the thief was after. Complexities of theft included conspiracy, which was punished more severely than a theft committed by a single thief. There are a number of passages which suggest that snitching on one's neighbour was not uncommon, an attitude reinforced by the administrative grouping of families into communities charged with mutual responsibility. However, excessive or inaccurate denunciation, exaggerating the amount stolen or accusing someone of stealing an ox when they'd only taken a sheep, was often punished by the heavy fine of a shield or two.

Killing a new-born baby with defects was not a crime but killing a baby because you had too many children already, was. The whole question of murder was dependent upon intention and method. Premeditated murder was punished more severely than accidental manslaughter. Beating an 'obstreperous' wife and breaking or dislocating her limbs was punished by shaving the man's beard off, one of a whole series of 'mutilation' punishments which ranged from beard- and head-shaving to tattooing and castration. Also in the category of punishment by shaving the beard off were fights in which noses or ears were bitten off, whilst cutting off a man's topknot in a fight was punished by hard labour without shaving or tattooing. In the case of bigamy, both the man and the second woman were tattooed and sentenced to hard labour. Taking a woman along in an official carriage incurred a heavy fine of two suits of armour. Arson leading to the destruction of a gate within a city meant a fine of a suit of armour, but if it was the main external city gate, two suits of armour were required. There is also a mysterious passage, apparently a quotation from a statute, which states, 'One must not venture to wear brocade shoes', although apparently plain shoes with brocade on the sides were acceptable.[12]

At the end of the 'Questions and Answers on the Law' are two longer passages which describe the investigation of two deaths. In one, a prefectural clerk was instructed to examine the body of a man. 'On the left corner of his neck was a wound made with a blade and on the back, two wounds … resembling wounds made by an axe.' His hemp skirt and jacket were stained with blood in places corresponding to the wounds, and a pair of silk shoes was found near the body. The shoes were put on his feet and were found to fit him. He was about 1.7 metres tall and his hair was nearly half a metre long. The clerk made enquiries of those living nearby to see if they had heard any noise on the night in question. The man was buried in his hemp skirt and his jacket and shoes were taken to the local government office, but we do not know if the case was resolved.[13]

The other case was that of a man found hanging in his own house. The prefectural clerk and a prison officer went to investigate. They examined the rope and described it in detail: it was looped twice round a rafter and knotted. The corpse was also examined and described: 'His tongue was level with his lips. Faeces and urine had been discharged, soiling both legs. When the rope was untied, the air of his mouth and neck escaped like a sigh.' The floor beneath the body was examined but there were no discernible footprints, so the body was released to his wife and daughter. This description of the investigation is followed by an explanation as to the importance of distinguishing suicide from murder disguised as suicide. The protruding tongue, the faeces and urine and the escape of air, as well the ease with which the rope could be released, all indicated suicide in this case. However, it was noted that 'people who commit suicide must have had reasons. Question the members of his household in order to have them reply concerning his reasons.'[14] In late imperial China suicide was sometimes used a method of blaming others: those who felt themselves seriously wronged might commit suicide in the house of their persecutor, who would be charged. It is possible that similar instances occurred in the Qin, hence the questioning of the household.[15]

These details of the Qin legal code and the instructions to legal officials suggest that the laws of Qin were not arbitrarily cruel, for

13. The death penalty

limits were set and circumstances considered when a case went to trial. Were the punishments excessively cruel? Prisoners might be beaten during interrogation, and beating was a common punishment. The death penalty meant beheading in the market place. Forced labour was a common punishment, often accompanied by various mutilations of which the least serious were merely markers of criminality such as shaving the head or the beard. Tattooing, which left a permanent reminder of a criminal act, was not unusual, and some criminals condemned to hard labour might also have their nose cut off, or their left foot (though that clearly rendered them useless as forced labour). The length of most sentences of forced labour is not specified, but the occasional reference to a six-year term indicates that most were for a shorter period.[16]

Officials were more likely to be fined than physically punished, being forced to pay for shields or suits of armour, and it appears that it was possible to redeem a punishment, presumably by paying a fine. It was certainly possible to redeem the punishment of castration: the Grand Scribe complained in 93 BC that he had had to suffer castration (for displeasing his emperor) because he had been unable to pay the fee that would have let him off.[17]

6

This Species of Fortification: The Great Wall

The First Emperor is commonly credited with the construction of the Great Wall, possibly the most enduring symbol of China. Snaking for hundreds of miles over the green hills north of Beijing, its grey battlements interrupted by tall grey watchtowers and narrow gates in the passes, for hundreds of years it has never failed to amaze visitors. The French Jesuit, Jean Baptiste du Halde (1674–1743), compiled a *Description géographique, historique, chronologique, politique de l'Empire de la Chine* (1735) which was based upon the detailed letters of his Jesuit confrères in China. The work contains numerous mentions of the Great Wall that speak of the engineering skill required to build it, its strategic significance and its imposing appearance. 'There is nothing in the World equal to this work,'[1] he notes in the first volume. A fuller description appears in the second volume in a chapter on the Chinese military:

Two hundred and fifteen years before the coming of Christ this prodigious work was built, by order of the First Emperor of the family of Qin to defend the three great provinces against the irruption of the Tartars.

As soon as he had determined on this grand Design, he drew a third part of the labouring men out of every province, and in order to lay the foundations of it on the sea coast, he commanded several vessels loaded with iron to be sunk to the bottom of the water, as likewise large stones, upon which the work was caused to be erected, with so much nicety and exactness that if the workmen left the least chasm discover-able between the stones, it was at the forfeit of their lives.

By this means the work is preserved to this day almost as entire as when it was new built ... It is hard to comprehend how this enormous Bulwark has been raised to the height we see it in dry barren places, where they were obliged to bring from a great distance, and with incredible labour, water, bricks, mortar and all the necessary materials for the construction of such a work.[2]

Thus was eighteenth-century Europe made aware of the Great Wall. Indeed it may have been such an account that stirred Dr Johnson in 1778 to talk to James Boswell,

with an uncommon animation of travelling into distant coun-tries; that the mind was enlarged by it, and that an acquisi-tion of dignity of character was derived from it. He expressed a particular enthusiasm with respect to visiting the Wall of China. I catched it for the moment and said I really believed I should go and see the Wall of China had I not children, of whom it was my duty to take care. 'Sir, (said he), by doing so, you would do what would be of importance in raising your children to eminence. There would be a lustre reflected upon them from your spirit and curiosity. They would be at all times regarded as the children of a man who had gone to view the Wall of China. I am serious, Sir.'[3]

In 1793, Lord Macartney, the first British Ambassador to China, wrote the first British eyewitness account of the Wall:

What the eye could, from a single spot, embrace of those fortified walls, carried along the ridges of hills, over the tops of the highest mountains, descending into the deepest valleys, crossing in arches over rivers, and doubled and trebled in many parts to take in important passes, and interspersed with towers or massy bastions at almost every hundred yards, as far as the sight could reach, presented to the mind an undertaking of stupendous magnitude ... This species of fortification, for to call it simply by the name of wall does not convey the idea of such a fabric, is described to extend, though not equally perfected throughout, in a course of fifteen hundred miles ...[4]

Lord Macartney knew little of early Chinese history, but on the subject of the Wall, the writer Jorge Luis Borges, who admitted that he would never see it, wrote, 'I read some days past, that the man who ordered the erection of the almost infinite wall of China was that first emperor, Shi huangdi, who also decreed that all books prior to him be burned. That these two vast operations – the five to six hundred leagues of stone opposing the barbarians, the rigorous abolition of history, that is of the past — should originate in one person and be in some way his attributes, in some way inexplicably satisfied and, at the same time, disturbed me.'[5] And in the sort of shorthand that is necessary when attempting to write a history of China from Peking Man to the twentieth century, the sinological historian C. P. Fitzgerald wrote, 'The Great Wall, though often repaired and refaced, was planned and linked together by Shi huangdi; although probably only the core of the modern wall is Qin work, the design and place of the wall were planned by the great Emperor, and subsequent generations have only restored or maintained his monument.'[6]

Lord Macartney was unaware that the Wall he saw, faced with brick and stone, was comparatively recent, built during the Ming, in the late sixteenth and early seventeenth centuries, whilst the accounts of Borges, Du Halde and Fitzgerald stress the ancient origin of the Wall and the involvement of the First Emperor. While there is no doubt that the First Emperor did order the construction of walls to the north of his territories, the history of the Great Wall is much more complicated than these writers would have us believe.

Wall-building in China antedates the activities of the First Emperor by several hundred years. During the Warring States period (481–221 BC), when the separate kingdoms in China were in a more or less permanent state of contention, defensive walls were built against neighbouring states, and the states on the periphery constructed boundary walls against their semi-settled and nomadic neighbours, creating 'a lattice of walls all over China'.[7]

The walls built by the early Qin state in the late fourth and early third centuries BC seem to have been built on the western and northern fringes, marking some kind of border against their non-Chinese neighbours. Once he had conquered the other states

71

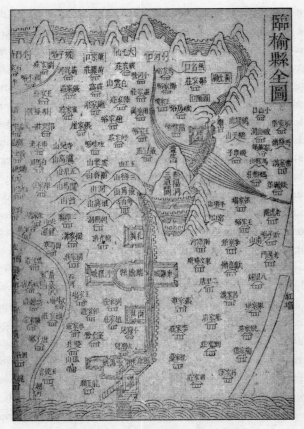

14. The Great Wall in Shandong province

and unified China, the First Emperor is recorded as sending General Meng north in 215 BC to attack the 'barbarians' and to take the land south of the northernmost line of the Yellow River. There, it is said, he 'built long walls, and constructed fortifications taking advantage of passes, according to the configuration of the terrain ... stretching over a distance of more than ten thousand li'.[8] 'Then he crossed the Yellow River and took possession of the Yang mountains which wind to the north like a snake.'[9]

The 'border' created by these walls was a complex one. By building the wall north of the Yellow River, the First Emperor incorporated the Ordos grasslands, inhabited by semi-nomadic peoples but not suited to Chinese agriculture. Though some have suggested that the northern walls were built to mark the separation between those who 'drew the bow' and inhabited the grasslands and those who 'wore the cap and girdle', the Chinese who tilled the fertile lands of the central plain, the incorporation of the Ordos contradicts this interpretation.[10] It seems more likely that the move north was part of the military offensive against northern, non-Chinese peoples and represented territorial expansion rather than simple border-marking.

The construction of walls and the consolidation of China effected by the First Emperor seem to have marked a change in cross-border relations. There were many separate groups living just beyond the Chinese states in the Warring States period. Nomadic, semi-nomadic or increasingly practising settled agriculture, they traded animals and furs with the Chinese for silk and other luxury goods. During the fourth century BC, there was a change in the emphasis on trade goods as the Chinese states sought to develop cavalry, not necessarily to ride against the northern barbarians but for state defence. It seems, also, that many of the peoples who lived closest to the Chinese were effectively absorbed. Indeed this was one of the accusations made against the state of Qin, that its people shared the customs of the barbarians and did not behave 'according to protocol, righteousness or virtuous action'.[11] The border tribes had been a form of buffer between China and the true nomads further north and it seems that the removal of this buffer, the increased wall-building activity of the First Emperor and his establishment of the Chinese state provoked a reaction amongst the nomads.

In response to General Meng's drive north, the nomads united to form the Xiongnu state under a ruler called Modun. According to legend, he gathered around him a formidable group of warriors. To test their loyalty, he ordered them to shoot his favourite horse, and executed all who disobeyed. Then he ordered them to shoot his favourite wife, with the same proviso. Finally, he ordered the remainder to shoot his father who had not wanted Modun to succeed him as tribal leader. Though the Xiongnu did not attack the Qin, when that dynasty fell, they became a major threat to the succeeding Han dynasty.

The First Emperor's wall-building activities probably consisted more in joining up and strengthening earlier walls such as that built by the Zhao in the area where General Meng was said to be building, and those erected by the local state of Yan north of Beijing. The sections of the Great Wall that still stand were rebuilt over centuries, and the work of rebuilding continues, so it is difficult to distinguish any Qin contribution, though some possible portions have been identified in Shaanxi, Ningxia, Gansu, Liaoning and Hebei provinces.[12]

Identification of the First Emperor's Great Wall is problematic, for several reasons. First, there is very little historical evidence. Apart from brief written references such as those to General Meng in *The Grand Scribe's Records*, no maps or plans survive, and the archaeological record is equally scanty. The Qin walls would have been made either of tamped earth or stones or a mixture of the two, according

15. Tamped earth or pisé *construction used for the Great Wall*

to what was locally available. Tamped earth or *pisé*, where earth is pounded in layers between wooden frames, produces remarkably long-lasting structures, for city walls 3,000 or more years old built by this method can still be seen in Zhengzhou, for example. Where the Great Wall has been rebuilt many times over the centuries, however, early pounded-earth layers would have been incorporated and hidden, and stones were frequently re-used.

Despite a lack of hard evidence, the association of the First Emperor with the Great Wall persists. The Chinese historian Zhu Tongjun wrote in 1957 that 'most people know' that the First Emperor built a Great Wall, but he admitted that he did not know whether the present Great Wall was that built on his orders.[13] Folklore credits the First Emperor with the construction of the Wall and emphasizes the cruelty involved. However and wherever the First Emperor's walls were built, they would have been constructed sometimes by corrupt officials sent north as punishment, sometimes by men serving as corvée labourers or on military service. All men of a certain age were compelled to offer themselves as labourers for a fixed period every three years, usually in their local area, building roads or canals, maintaining dykes and public buildings. If they failed to do so, they were punished with the bastinado.[14] It is probable that wall-building on and beyond the northern frontier was done by men serving their military service, when out of the three years they might be expected to serve on the frontier in the second year.[15]

According to a folk story first recorded in the fifteenth century but perhaps at least partly based on a story recorded in the first century BC, General Meng died far away from home after building the Great Wall. Such was his wife's distress at his death so far away and the consequent impossibility of bringing his body home for burial that she travelled to the spot where he died and her tears made a section of the Great Wall crumble. His selfless contribution and her devotion are commemorated in a temple built near where the Great Wall meets the sea at Shanhaiguan.[16]

Closer in time, a sacrifice to the Wall demanded by the son of the First Emperor was recorded in *The Grand Scribe's Records*. Though these *Records* are almost invariably intensely critical of the First Emperor and his successor, and everything they did, their account of the fate of General Meng, revealing the perils of serving under a new emperor as a known favourite of his predecessor, is relatively impartial. After listing his achievements in road- and wall-building and as a military leader, the account continues with an order written in the name of the deceased First Emperor by those who had placed the Second Emperor on the throne, that General Meng commit suicide. Though he took several years to accede, in one of the first recorded references to a crime against *feng shui*, General Meng said, 'I built walls and dug moats for more than ten thousand *li*; was it not inevitable that I broke the earth's veins along the way? This then is my offence.' He then swallowed poison and killed himself.[17]

The Burning of the Books

Veneration of the written word is characteristic of traditional China. The art of writing was, during the Ming (1368–1644) at least, rated higher than painting, so a piece of good calligraphy cost more than a painting.[1] It was not just the form of the writing that was significant but also its content. For well over two thousand years, the acquisition of a library, containing historical archives and literary works, was a priority of rulers, and these gatherings of texts allowed the development of commentary or exegesis. As Paul Demieville has put it, 'The history of Confucianism is the history of exegesis.' He noted too that in the (lost) commentaries of the earlier Han (210 BC–AD 6) on the works of Confucius, it was said that 'sometimes as many as twenty or thirty thousand characters were used to gloss a passage of five characters'.[2] It is clear from this volume of commentary that texts were considered to be of great importance, and the struggle to interpret them gave rise to considerable debate.

In that context, the 'burning of the books' by the First Emperor was traditionally viewed as a terrible act of censorship and cultural vandalism. According to *The Grand Scribe's Records*, in 213 BC the First Emperor held a banquet at the palace attended by a hundred scholars. At the banquet one scholar criticized the establishment of a civil administration and the First Emperor's failure to offer land and territory to his relatives as had been done in the past (with disastrous results). He continued, 'I have yet to hear of anything able to endure that was not based on ancient precedents.'

In response, the Councillor noted that times had changed: 'Your Majesty has built up this great empire to endure for generations without end. Naturally,' he added, 'this passes the comprehension of a foolish pedant.' He criticized scholars who 'use their learning to oppose our rule ... using empty rhetoric ... to slander the laws ... and incite the mob to spread rumours'. The Councillor's answer to the pedants was to propose that all the historical records but those of Qin be burned:

> If anyone who is not a court scholar dares to keep the ancient songs, historical records or writings of the hundred schools, these should be confiscated and burned by the provincial governor and army commander. Those who in conversation dare to quote the old songs and records should be publicly executed; those who use old precedents to oppose the new order should have their families wiped out; and officers who know of such cases but fail to report them should be punished in the same way.
>
> If thirty days after the issuing of this order, the owners of these books still have not had them destroyed, they should have their faces tattooed and be condemned to hard labour at the Great Wall. The only books which need not be destroyed are those dealing with medicine, divination and agriculture.[3]

16. The burning of the books

These proposals, together with the assumption that they were carried out to the letter, have traditionally been interpreted as a wholesale attack on Confucianism and literature, borne out of a desire to create a *tabula rasa* by eliminating the past (except where it concerned the history of Qin) and all opposition. In a society that, after the Qin, became increasingly dominated by respect for books and scholars, this was regarded as one of the First Emperor's worst acts.

Closer examination of the Councillor's list shows that he did not intend the wholesale elimination of proscribed books, for 'court scholars' were still allowed to possess or read them. Instead he singled out the historical records of the other Warring States for elimination in an evident attempt to wipe them from history. He also mentioned by name two books closely connected with Confucian thought, the *Book of Songs* and the *Book of History*.[4] Both were counted amongst the Five Confucian Classics. The *Book of History* consists of 'semi-historical documents and speeches dating from the early centuries of the Zhou period' (c. 1025–481 BC) and its contents would have been as unpopular with the Councillor as the records of the other states, for they provided dissident scholars with precisely the sort of 'old precedents to oppose the new order' which he wished to avoid. As has been noted in an earlier chapter, from the fifth century BC, as the country was beset by endemic war, scholars and thinkers tended to look back to the legendary rulers of the past whose time in retrospect became a peaceful golden age. Even the Grand Scribe made it clear that his historical *Records* were intended, in the right hands, as an instrument to 'rectify the world' through reference to past glories, as well as the mistakes made by former rulers.[5]

The *Book of Songs*, traditionally but inaccurately said to have been collected by Confucius, is a less obvious choice. A collection of 305 songs dating from roughly the tenth to the seventh century BC, it includes some political verses, though many are love songs or songs about the rhythm of the agricultural year, containing many references to plants, birds and the seasonal cycle. It may have been this political association, as well as the antiquity of the songs, that provoked the ban.

Though most assume that an actual book-burning of some sort did take place, it is probable that it was the use to which books were put and the subversive activities of scholars that most preoccupied the Councillor. It has been argued that what is usually translated as 'the writings of the hundred schools' and understood as all existing philosophical writing, should actually be understood as 'compilations of didactic historical anecdotes', in effect, popular compilations of stories about the past, rather similar in content to the *Book of History* and seen by the Councillor as subversive in precisely the same way, for they provided ammunition for the discontented to suggest that the First Emperor was wrong to break with the past and that everything had been better in some distant ancestral world.[6]

The books that were exempted from destruction were largely practical manuals devoted to medicine and agriculture, although the First Emperor's own interest in portents and immortality may have been reflected in the preservation of works on divination. It is interesting to note that in the grave of the legal official discovered at the Place of the Sleeping Tiger were found two books of divination.[7] These bamboo-slip books listed auspicious days for different activities and, like Chinese almanacs today, also included mention of the cycle of twelve animals, the earliest reference to a cycle that still plays its part in Chinese horoscopes today.[8]

It is impossible to estimate now how many books were actually lost. The destruction by fire of the Qin imperial library when the palaces were burned by the Han in 206 BC was probably of far greater significance.[9] What is more, a surviving catalogue of the Han imperial library made around the time of the birth of Christ includes a list of titles of which over three-quarters no longer exist, suggesting that the subsequent destruction of books at various times was equally devastating.[10]

Were scholars killed at the same time or were they simply tattooed and sent off to build the Great Wall? *The Emperor's Mirror* was an illustrated account of 'good' and 'bad' emperors produced for the education of the young Wanli emperor (r. 1572–1620) who had ascended the throne at the age of nine. It includes a picture of a pile of books being burned under the supervision of the First Emperor whilst scholars are tipped into a pit to be buried alive.[11] The death of the scholars is noted in the *Grand Scribe's Records*, where it states that in 212 BC, despite the burning of the books, the First Emperor was angered by the continuing resistance of scholars. 'I collected all the writings of the empire and got rid of those which were no use. I assembled a host of scholars and alchemists to start a reign of peace, hoping the alchemists would find marvellous herbs ... Handsomely as I treated ... the scholars, they are libelling me, making out that I lack virtue.'[12] Fearing that the scholars' accusations would affect the ordinary people and incite revolt, he had the scholars tried by the Councillor: they apparently 'incriminated each other in order to save their own necks'. Over 460 scholars were executed in the capital.

Accounts of the method of execution vary according to the reading of a crucial Chinese character usually now interpreted as meaning 'buried alive'. This is the interpretation that appears in

The Emperor's Mirror, but some suggest a more complex version by which the First Emperor summoned the scholars to admire 'unusual winter-blooming melons', whereupon they fell into a hidden pit dug beneath the melons.[13] More recent research suggests that the character has been misread and that it should simply mean 'killed', by a method unspecified.[14] More significantly, a probable eyewitness, a scholar who survived to advise the first emperor of the Han dynasty through enumeration of the mistakes of the First Emperor, particularly his preference for law and punishment over the Confucian virtues of 'benevolence' and 'righteousness', never mentioned either the burning of the books or the killing of his fellow-scholars.

It is likely that the legend grew up as a result of a fierce battle between two groups of Confucian scholars, on the one side those of the New Text school who maintained that the burning of the books meant that the whole Confucian canon had to be reassembled and reinterpreted, and on the other the Old Text school who claimed to have discovered a version of the canon in the ancestral home of Confucius himself. In order to escape the burning of the books it had been hidden in a hollow brick wall which has subsequently become an object of veneration known as the Lu Wall.

Whilst it seems clear that the First Emperor and his Councillor sought to eliminate opposition, particularly scholarly opposition spread by rumour, it seems likely that both the 'burning of the books' and the 'burying of the scholars' attributed to the First Emperor and contributing hugely to his posthumous reputation for cruelty and megalomania, were greatly exaggerated.

Though the First Emperor is known almost uniquely in Chinese history for his destructive censorship, others have been as guilty. An emperor of the Song dynasty burned the collected works of three

17. *The burial of the scholars*

poets in 1103, and the first emperor of the Mongol Yuan dynasty, Kublai Khan, twice ordered the burning of Daoist books and woodblocks in 1258 and 1281.

The great Qianlong emperor of the Qing (r. 1736–96) was equally culpable. In 1772, he issued an edict proposing the collection of all extant texts for the imperial library to preserve them against 'future loss' and to enable the compilation of a massive encyclopaedic work, the *Complete Collections of the Four Treasuries*.[15] The Emperor's grandfather, the Kangxi emperor, had ordered the compilation of another sort of encyclopaedic work, the *Synthesis of Books and Illustrations of Ancient and Modern Times*, which was printed from copper movable type in 1722. Its 10,000 slim volumes contained quotations from earlier works arranged by subject and often accompanied by illustrations.[16] The Qianlong emperor's plan was more ambitious, for instead of extracts, he wanted to produce complete copies of all the works collected. The *Complete Collections of the Four Treasuries*, comprising 36,000 volumes, was not printed but copied out in manuscript, in seven separate sets, between 1782 and 1787.

The project might, on the surface, seem admirable in its desire to preserve literature, but behind it lay a much-resented policy and an even more sinister inquisition. One scholar refused to hand over a unique collection of his great-grandfather's poems and was sentenced to be beaten with 100 strokes and sent into exile for three years. What is more, as the poems were pronounced seditious, his great-grandfather's body was dug up and dismembered in a posthumous punishment.[17] Works collected from willing or unwilling bibliophiles were examined. The Qing, who were Manchu not Chinese, had had to expend considerable military force to conquer China, and pockets of loyal supporters of the defeated (Chinese) dynasty of the Ming held out for some decades. The Qing sensitivity at being non-Chinese was extended to criticisms of earlier non-Chinese rulers such as the Mongols and the several short-lived non-Chinese dynasties that had ruled in the north in the thirteenth and early fourteenth centuries. There was also sensitivity about works dealing with the strategically significant but often turbulent border areas. In addition, it seems that the Qianlong emperor's book-collectors were style policemen, ready to suppress works that were unliterary and described varyingly as 'lying nonsense', 'language and ideas turbid and confused', 'its language ... very vulgar ... exaggerated and absurd in places ... fiction'.[18]

The greatest imperial sensitivity, however, concerned criticism of the imperial house and its members, a sensitivity amounting almost to paranoia. One scholar was reported as having been sent in 1726 to Jiangxi to conduct the provincial or second-level examinations that would select educated men for service in the imperial bureaucracy (which had been established by the First Emperor nearly 2,000 years earlier). The examinations required candidates to write highly stylized essays on topics invariably taken from the Confucian Classics. In this case, the text proposed for the essay was a simple four-character phrase from the *Great Learning*, 'Where the people rest'. The candidates might have complained about this gnomic and somewhat ambivalent phrase but someone made a far more serious accusation, pointing out that the first and last characters were similar to those of the reign title of the emperor's own father, but without the top parts. In other words, the scholar was subtly suggesting that the emperor's father should have been decapitated. The scholar was seized and thrown into prison. Further searches of his house apparently revealed diaries containing more seditious comments. The scholar died in prison but his body was dismembered after death as an extra punishment. In an echo of the mutual responsibility system that existed during the time of the First Emperor, his brothers were also imprisoned, one dying in prison, the other shortly after he was released.[19]

The Qianlong emperor's ruthless collection of books, 'flagrant disregard for the rights of private ownership'[20] and brutal punishment of scholars and bibliophiles resulted in the destruction or substantial alteration of 2,665 works and the death and dismemberment of over a hundred scholars – a far more systematic expunging of records than the First Emperor's alleged burning of books and burial of scholars.

In recent times, too, China's rulers have made efforts to censor the records. Chairman Mao may not have ordered the destruction of books, but during the Cultural Revolution, vast quantities of works published before 1966 were withdrawn from library shelves, making them in effect inaccessible to a whole generation of scholars. Students at Beijing University required a chit from a teacher to be allowed access to 'forbidden' texts, even back numbers of journals such as *Historical Research*, published in the 1950s. The open catalogues in the university library contained no cards for 'forbidden' works and they could only be seen through application to the librarians and with permission.

8

Making Everything the Same

The First Emperor's approach to diversity has been described by one scholar as fundamentally an attempt to 'standardize the mind of his people as he had previously standardized weights and measures'.[1] The standardization of physical things — cart-axles, roads, weights and measures, the written script and the coinage — that was carried out by order of the First Emperor is one aspect of his rule that has not come in for much criticism, although it has not been praised either.

Standardization of the coinage after the establishment of the empire in 221 BC made economic sense but it was also essential for the smooth running of the new bureaucratic administration. Though there were various forms of money used from 221 BC, the most significant introduction was the basic bronze coin, circular with a square hole in the middle, a form which was to endure until the late nineteenth century and which became another essential element of Chinese culture. During the Qin, coins were inscribed with two characters giving the theoretical weight of the coin, the equivalent of 8 grammes. Though some coins that have been excavated do weigh 8 grammes, others show substantial variations in weight. It

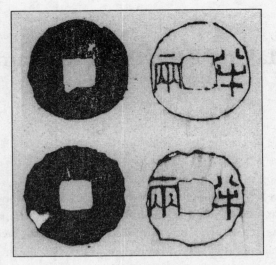

18. Qin coins

is therefore probable that the coin's value lay in its inscription rather than the monetary value of the metal used. This basic coin had a value of 1, and it seems that 1,000 coins was also an accounting unit as special containers for 1,000 coins have been excavated.

From the bamboo-slip documents found at the Place of the Sleeping Tiger, which provide us with so much information on the laws and administration under the First Emperor, we know that all items for sale in the market with a value of one coin or more had to be labelled. And though other forms of money, such as textiles, were used, their value was still reckoned in coin, with one piece of textile money (1.85 × 0.52 metres) considered the equivalent of 11 coins (multiples of 11 are often found in administrative documents). Labour costs were counted in coins, with the price of one day's labour being the equivalent of 8 coins. And though the fines paid by administrators who had failed in their tasks were usually stated in shields, the fine could be paid in the coin equivalent to the value of one shield, that is 5,000 coins.[2]

This streamlined new coinage system was implemented throughout the empire, replacing an extraordinary variety of currency that had existed before. The earliest form of currency in China seems to have been cowrie shells, followed in the Bronze Age by coinage in the shape of spades, often cast with a hollow cylinder at the top, like a real metal spade blade. Spade coins came in a variety of forms, with square shoulders and straight, pointed or forked tips. Not long before the unification of China, one state issued coins cast in the form of knives, another issued bronze cowries and yet another issued small gold plaques with impressed inscriptions. There were also round coins with round holes and round coins with square holes in different states. Despite their variety of form, all were produced in multiple pottery moulds.

Whilst coins in theory represented a specific weight or value, though the actual weight varied, the standardization of weights and measures, another of the First Emperor's unifying innovations, was a matter of far greater precision. This becomes evident from the group of 'Statutes of Checking' found at the Place of the Sleeping Tiger under the belly of the corpse of the official interred there. The twenty-nine statutes make it clear that officials were responsible for checking weights and measures and were held accountable if these were inaccurate. If the official grain measure was out by 16 ounces or more, the official in charge was fined a suit of armour; if it was inaccurate by less than 16 ounces, he was fined one shield. Even the suits of armour held in government stores were checked and had to

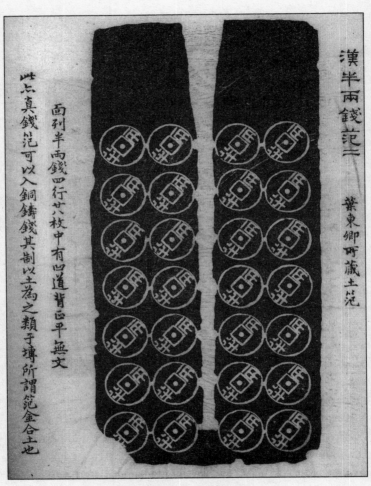

漢半兩錢范三　葉東卿所藏土范

面列半兩錢四行共枚中有四道背□平無文

此□真錢范可以入銅鑄錢其制以土為之類于博所謂范金合土也

19. *Moulds for casting coins*

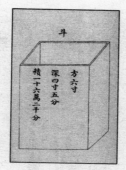

20. A dou *measuring vessel*

be made good if they were not of the standard quality (measured by the number of small 'scales' of leather).[3]

The equipment used by the First Emperor's officials to measure and assess grain and other materials included measuring vessels made of clay or bronze, the latter either circular or rectangular. They were all marked, inscribed or incised with seals recording an edict of 221 BC: 'In the 26th year, the emperor completely unified the lords of the empire. The common people were at ease. And he was designated sovereign emperor. He issued an edict ... [that] standardized measurements. When they are not uniform or are in doubt, make them uniform.'

These vessels were made to measure capacity and were used in measuring tax collected in grain and to dole out rations to workers on government projects. Male workers building walls or roads were given a morning meal of half a *dou* of grain and an evening meal of a third of a *dou*. Women set the same task were given two meals of a third of a *dou* a day. Quite what a *dou* was is difficult to assess: though the Chinese have used the same terms for measurements ever since,

21. *A weight to be hung on a measuring scale*

the equivalents have varied greatly over the centuries. Today's *dou* is a decalitre, made up of ten *sheng*, though there appear to have been eight *sheng* to a *dou* in Qin, although in one classical text a *dou* is glossed differently. One contemporary scholar gives the size rather than the weight equivalent of a *dou* as approximately 200 centimetres.[4]

Apart from measures of volume for weighing out rations, the First Emperor's officials also used measures of weight. These were made of bronze and were semi-spherical in shape, with a pierced knob at the top, and were presumably hung from the sort of hand-held measuring scales that can still be seen in Chinese markets. These latter take the form of a rod, marked with notches, with a hook at one end from which goods or a small brass tray to hold smaller items are hung. The weight is moved along the other end until a balance is achieved. The Qin weights are, like their capacity-measuring counterparts, inscribed with the edict of 221 BC and they come in various sizes of *jin*, nowadays a weight of half a kilo but apparently about 254 grammes during the Qin. Standard weights to the equivalent of 1, 5, 10, 15, 20, 30, 60 and 120 *jin* have been excavated.[5]

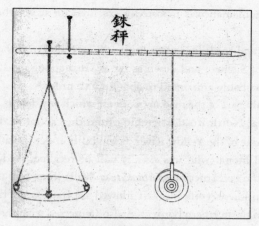

鈇
秤

22. *A hand-held measuring scale*

The standardization of chariot axles and the construction of roads were closely interlinked. Using forced labour and conscript labour, the First Emperor had a network of roads, carefully prepared with rubble and pounded-earth surfaces, and lined with ditches and pine trees, built across his new empire. After a tour of inspection, bumping along poor roads in 220 BC, he ordered the construction of a set of 'speed ways' radiating out from the capital to the north, north-east, south and south-east.[6] These were not merely for his own convenience but also improved communications with the more distant parts of his empire and allowed for fast travel by the official carts and runners carrying essential government information to the capital. The 'speed ways' were probably about forty feet wide (and therefore broader than their Roman counterparts). The central lanes of the roads were reserved for the emperor and his family, with everyone else, including the government runners, using the outer lanes. A nobleman was reportedly executed for using the middle lane.[7]

Less grand roads, narrower in width, extended into the western province of Sichuan and down as far as Guangdong, and the total network probably amounted to about 4,250 miles.[8]

The only part of the road network for which any details are given is the Great North Road, stretching from the capital to the northernmost edge of the Yellow River. It was built under the supervision of General Meng (who was also, it will be recalled, credited with much of the construction of the Great Wall) from 212 BC. Apart from its military significance – it allowed fast transport of troops and supplies to the northern border – it also connected with the territory of the northern barbarians, allowing observation of their activities as well as trade.[9]

Before the construction of the Great North Road but at about the time the First Emperor ordered the 'speed way' network, it was also decreed that all chariot axles throughout the empire should be made to a uniform size, a 'double pace' or six feet, thought to be the equivalent of about 4.71 feet today.[10] Some say that this standardization made it easier for carts and chariots to follow the deep ruts that inevitably developed even on the best-made roads, but one does wonder how they ever got out of the ruts and off the main road.

Another of the major cultural contributions of the First Emperor was the standardization of the written script. In effect, he and his Councillor imposed a style and system of writing Chinese characters that has, with very little alteration, persisted to this day. Had they not imposed such standardization, it is possible that different areas of China where different dialects were spoken would have developed their own scripts. As it is, a single script covering a massive country where spoken dialects differ greatly has held the country together for over 2,000 years. Today the script is universally understood although spoken dialects vary hugely. If someone from Guangdong were to read a passage aloud in his own dialect, his pronunciation would be incomprehensible to an inhabitant of Beijing (and vice versa). Yet the written text itself would be comprehensible to both. In today's world, where radio and television are significant means of communication, it is possible to impose a standard spoken language, 'common speech', that can be taught to all children. In the past, however, it was the script that united and informed all Chinese, whatever dialect they spoke.

Fundamentally, a Chinese character represents a word (though in today's Chinese many 'words' consist of two characters or more). The earliest surviving characters were inscribed on bones and tortoise shells and record the divination questions of the Shang kings (*c.* 1200 BC). Subsequent kingdoms have left inscriptions incised or impressed on bronze vessels. By the time of the Warring States (475–221 BC) it seems that different states were using different characters, probably reflecting different local pronunciations of words.[11] Considerable evidence of local variation can be seen in a silk manuscript dating to *c.* 300 BC found in a tomb at Changsha in a southern state. This contains an 'appreciably large number of "descentless graphs"' or characters which did not survive the First Emperor's standardization.[12] It has been suggested that these 'descentless graphs' represented the regional nature of the local 'written' dialect, which in turn probably represented the local spoken dialect.

The Councillor and his advisors seem to have favoured graphs comprising combinations of elements, ancestors of today's characters which, in dictionaries, are arranged by 214 'radicals' plus the

23. A Qin inscription in 'small seal' script

rest of the character. It is possible that the new favoured characters reflected changes in pronunciation which meant that the phonetic element of a character had largely lost its significance. About a quarter of all pre-existing characters were eliminated and it is presumed that forms used in Qin itself predominated. The style of the characters also reflected the style used in Qin, known as 'small seal' script.

Though the style of writing characters changed in the subsequent Han dynasty in favour of a clearer, clerical style, virtually the same as that used today, the standardization of the script and of the form of characters under the First Emperor laid the basis for a real unification of language throughout China.

9

The Supreme Forest and the Hall of 10,000 Guests

The earliest rulers in northern China enjoyed hunting and had land cleared on a grand scale to establish parks in which to do so. The extravagance of the hunts and other entertainments held in these great parks, and the creation of the parks themselves, were often used to characterize 'bad' rulers. The last rulers of some of the semi-mythical early dynasties, responsible for the fall of their ruling house, were attacked for squandering the royal treasury on gardens built for orgies. The last ruler of the Yin dynasty, who is said to have died in 1122 BC, 'constructed a vast pleasaunce ... in which there was a lake of wine and a garden with meat hanging on the trees. There all kinds of the wildest orgies were carried on, until he was finally overthrown ... and perished in the flames of his palace.'[1] It was not just these extravagances that were criticized. The creation of such parks also damaged the livelihood of the ordinary people. According to the Confucian philosopher Mencius, such rulers 'set aside the cultivated fields, and made gardens and animal preserves of them, so that the common people could not obtain clothing and food ... With an abundance of gardens and preserves, of puddles and pools, of fens and lakes, the birds and beasts came.' Mencius felt that mankind's needs should come before those of animals and wildfowl.[2]

'Good' rulers, by contrast, used their parks 'for raising dragons' – dragons were seen as beneficent creatures – or employed the results of the hunt as offerings in ancestral temples, thus maintaining the essential rituals that held family and nation together. According to Mencius, in the golden past, ordinary people had been allowed into royal parks 'to gather fuel and catch hares and pheasants', whereas the rulers he saw about him excluded common people from their parks.[3] To keep the common people out and to maintain a steady supply of meat for sacrifices and to feed state guests, the parks were run by park officials and guarded, apparently, by criminals supplied by the public executioner – foot amputees are particularly mentioned, though one suspects they may have had some difficulty hopping about in pursuit of intruders.[4]

We have no idea of the actual size of these hunting preserves. Those owned by local rulers in the Warring States period may have been smaller than those of their predecessors, but we know that they were large enough to allow rulers to hunt geese and deer and that they included lakes – one annal records concubines teasing their lord by rocking his boat as it floated on the lake.[5] Whatever their size, they included all the essential ingredients: space to hunt, lakes for ducks, geese and pleasure boats, and buildings that included temples for sacrifices.

The First Emperor had one such enclosure constructed on the south side of the Wei River, opposite the capital. He called it Shanglin, the 'Supreme Forest', and it has become one of the symbols of the excess of his rule. Nothing remains of the Supreme Forest today, partly because the Wei River has scoured it away and partly because the succeeding Han dynasty is said to have returned the land to local farmers. This gesture to the farmers was less generous than it seemed, for the Han emperors had their own vast hunting parks enclosed elsewhere.

The earliest Chinese dictionary, the *Explanation of Single Component Graphs and Analyses of Complex Characters*, completed in AD 100, glosses the character which we now use for 'garden' as meaning 'a forest', which suggests that the gardens of the time were larger and more wooded than those of later periods.[6] With nothing remaining of the Supreme Forest, we do not know what the buildings in it were like, or whether artificial mountains were built up, and artificial lakes and ponds dug out, as in later Chinese gardens. It may well be that, apart from native fauna such as deer, geese and ducks, exotic animals were also kept in the Supreme Forest, for the succeeding Han emperors regarded their own 'Supreme Forest' (unusually, they retained the name) as a 'replica of all under Heaven' and stocked it with animals from distant parts of China such as yaks, elephants, rhinoceroses and a 'black, bear-like bamboo eater'. They also held Roman-style competitions in which men wrestled and fought with lions, leopards and bears.[7]

It is difficult to know what sort of plants, apart from trees, might have grown in the Supreme Forest. Those mentioned in the *Book of Songs* (compiled between the tenth and seventh centuries BC) include the peony, an emblem of love exchanged between girls and boys, bamboos of all sorts, roses, orchids and chrysanthemums (the emblem of autumn). Other plants are harder to identify because they had different names in different places and at different times so that even early Chinese botanists of the third and fourth centuries

AD were sometimes unsure exactly what was meant by a particular name in the ancient *Book of Songs*.[8]

The problem is even greater in translation, for as one authority has remarked, 'the great sinologists of modern times, preoccupied more with the literature than the botany, made heavy weather of it'.[9] The water gentian mentioned in the *Book of Songs* was variously translated as 'duckweed' and 'water mallow', which puts it in the wrong family. Similarly, the creeper *Metaplexis japonica* was translated as 'sedge' or 'sparrow-gourd', a name also applied to it in ancient times but which associates it wrongly with gourds in the Cucurbitae group, and 'vine-bean', which makes it a legume rather than a member of the family of Asclepidae.[10]

The closest we are likely to get to a description of the Supreme Forest of the First Emperor is a description of the subsequent Supreme Forest of the Han dynasty in a poem written in the second century BC. This starts with a description of natural rivers channelled into the park which rushed through chasms, boiled in gorges, wound round islets and meandered through groves of cinnamon trees before flowing into great lakes and pools. The pools were filled with 'sturgeon and salamanders, carp, bream, dudgeon and dace, cowfish, flounder and sheatfish' as well as turtles and 'horned dragons and red hornless dragons'.[11] Floating on the water above the fish and dragons were 'wild geese and swans, graylags, bustards, cranes and mallards, loons and spoonbills, teals and gadwalls, grebes, night herons and cormorants ... gobbling at the reeds and duckweed, pecking at water chestnuts and lotuses'.[12]

Below the park's towering mountain peaks with their blanket of densely packed trees, the lake banks and dykes were 'blanketed with green orchids' and a 'vast and unbroken mass of flowers': snake-

24. *A natural river channelled into a park*

mouth, magnolias, yucca, sedge, bittersweet, gentians, blue flags, ginger, turmeric, monkshood, wolfsbane, nightshade, basil, mint, ramie and blue artemisia. The park contained a similarly rich mix of trees, some growing by the buildings, others on the mountains: citrons, bitter oranges, limes, loquats, persimmons, wild pears, tamarinds, jujubes, cherries, almonds, damsons, crab apples, chestnuts, willows, birch, maples, sycamores, pomegranates, cedars and cypresses.[13]

The banks of the waters and the caves dug into the mountain peaks were described as glistening with garnets, green jade, coral, agate, marble, rose quartz, rock crystal, opals, pearls and chrysoberyl, and the park was filled with herds of water buffalo, yaks, tapirs, elephants, rhinoceroses, wild asses, camels, donkeys and, to keep the dragons company, unicorns.[14] In the hills were black and white apes, baboons and flying squirrels, lemurs, langurs, macaques and gibbons 'dwelling among the trees'. The Emperor in his ivory chariot followed hunters after leopards, panthers, jackals, wolves, bears, wild sheep, deer and boars whilst archers shot white-feathered arrows at pheasants, peacocks, black cranes and (along with the dragons and unicorns) phoenixes.

On the lake, the Emperor relaxed in a pelican boat propelled by servants with poles, and in the evening he ordered wine to be brought to the Terrace of Azure Heaven where he was entertained by performances of ancient music played on racks of bells and drums, by singing girls, dancers, actors and 'trained dwarfs'.[15]

It is clear from the poem that there were numerous buildings in the Supreme Forest, and architecture remained a major feature of later Chinese parks and gardens. Apart from the Terrace of Azure Heaven, presumably an open terrace beside a lake, there were palaces

25. *A terrace for gazing at a distant prospect*

for the Emperor and his guests to stay in, including the Palace of Righteous Spring and the Wild Plum Palace, and dwellings decorated with wind-chimes for the palace women, shaded and screened by trees. Quite a number of the buildings mentioned were clearly the ancestors of later garden pavilions, the Great Peak Tower, the Magpie Turret and the Cold Dew Observatory, all designed to offer magnificent views over lakes and mountains.[16]

As a physical description of the First Emperor's vanished Supreme Forest, a poem describing another imperial park a hundred years later is not very satisfactory, and the picture is complicated by its piling up of riches, with gemstones bordering lakes and lining caves, and the inclusion of dragons and phoenixes amongst the lists of real animals. However, architectural styles appear not to have changed dramatically during the intervening century, and the general impression of a massive and extravagant enclosure designed to provide entertainment of all sorts for the Emperor conveys something of what the vanished Supreme Forest must have been like.

Concrete evidence of the First Emperor's architectural activities is similarly lacking. According to *The Grand Scribe's Records*, the first constructions in 220 BC were imperial ancestral temples which were of vital significance to the ruling house and hence the empire, followed by the Palace of the Illustrious Terrace and the Supreme Forest, all on the southern bank of the Wei River, opposite the capital. North of the capital a series of buildings were constructed in the hills, replicas of the palaces of each of the states that the First Emperor had conquered, expressing his domination of the empire in physical form.

To the east of the capital, outside the east gate, a series of 'courts, walled-in avenues and pavilions' were constructed to house the

成造木子圖

26. *Carpenters at work*

beautiful women and musical instruments captured during the wars of conquest.[17] The 'walled-in avenues' may have been elevated and it is likely that covered walkways linked the buildings. The population of the capital itself was greatly increased when the First Emperor ordered that 120,000 wealthy families from all over the empire move to the capital, where they must have occupied fine residences.

On his travels through his realm, the First Emperor set up stone stelae in fine pavilions on the top of sacred mountains. Since he spent so much time travelling, it has been suggested that he may have constructed several hundred 'travelling palaces' to stay in on his excursions. These would have been strictly for imperial use and would have remained empty at all other times. Scant remains of a couple of 'travelling palaces' have been unearthed on the north-east coast, revealing pounded-earth foundations, various types of brick tiles, some with stamped decoration, and roof tiles.[18]

It has also been suggested that the proliferation of palaces constructed by the First Emperor both around the capital and further afield was not simply a result of his habit of travelling but a consequence of advice from advisors on drugs of immortality, known as recipe gentlemen. One advised that if he wished to achieve longevity he should move around frequently and keep his whereabouts as secret as possible. This was perhaps a better method of ensuring long life after three assassination attempts than that offered by other recipe gentlemen – that he ingest 'fire stone' and 'cold powder' pills.

What is certain is that the First Emperor received an enormous amount of advice from such men, some of it contradictory and none of it successful. During the Warring States period, there were many local rulers and aristocrats to employ them but when the First Emperor defeated all his rivals, there was only one court in which they could seek employment, so they all converged upon the First Emperor.[19] He is recorded as being angry when he saw the vast retinue of the Councillor that had followed him to his Cold Mountain Palace. Though the Councillor immediately reduced the size of his retinue, the First Emperor had most of his own retinue executed when he failed to find out who had informed the Councillor of his whereabouts. It may have been to prevent people knowing his exact whereabouts that he ordered the construction of concealing, covered walkways linking his palaces.

Palace building continued around the capital. In 220, the Palace of Trust was built on the south side of the Wei River, but almost immediately the First Emperor decided that it should become a temple instead and he named it the Paramount Temple, representing the Pole Star, an imperial symbol. This suggests that grand architecture of the period could be multi-purpose, although, given the First Emperor's reputation for extravagant construction, the change in use might in fact have involved considerable transformation.[20]

Excavations near his capital have revealed two palace buildings, though experts cannot agree on which palaces they were. The grandest is an L-shaped construction 60 metres wide, 45 metres deep and two storeys high, with the upper level raised 6 metres above the lower level. Such raised structures were created by the formation of a massive pounded-earth terrace. The buildings on the lower level were necessarily smaller and narrower as they were confined by the great central mound. On the top level was a huge hall positioned at the centre of the terrace with a large pillar in the middle, which, together with subsidiary columns around the edge of the building, supported the roof. The hall is thought to have been the imperial

27. *Officials approach a multi-storeyed hall*

audience hall, with room for the palace guards at the back, whilst a smaller hall to the right may have been the First Emperor's living quarters. On the lower level were five chambers with bathing rooms which may have been where the palace women lived. Both levels were surrounded by covered walkways and, to the north, there was access to a covered walk that encircled the whole palace. The L-shaped form, unlike the usual plan of enclosed courtyards, suggests that there might have been an identical building to the east, which would have created the usual symmetry, but no trace of it has yet been found.[21]

In another nearby palace compound, the remains of wall paintings that may have lined arcaded walkways have been found. They include 'delicate renderings of figures, horses and carriages and trees in red, black, blue, green, yellow, white and other colours' depicting court life at the time.

Palace building took place on a grand scale in and around the Supreme Forest in 212 BC. The most impressive structure was a massive audience hall. It is thought that this was only a part of a gigantic palace which remained unfinished at the time of the First Emperor's death two years later. This palace's name is rendered Apang, Epang or O-p'ang, and the interpretations of its meaning are as varied as its names. Many translate it as meaning the 'Nearby Palace', though that is hardly a name with imperial associations, while others believe it refers to a place-name. The most satisfactory explanation is that it was a temporary name and that it means 'Hipped Roof Hall', referring to the only part that was built during the First Emperor's lifetime.[22]

The new palace complex was linked to the capital on the north bank of the Wei River by a bridge which was also described as a covered walkway, conjuring a vision of a form of Rialto Bridge, with red columns and roof and, perhaps, painted panels all the way along it. It was also described in symbolic terms as linking the Pole Star with the Royal Chamber, passing over the Milky Way (the Wei River).[23]

Two different literary accounts state that the hall was either 675 metres east to west and 112 metres north to south or 1,350 metres east to west and 400 metres north to south. Like the other excavated palace foundations, it was a two-storey structure with a massive pounded-earth terrace raising the upper storey high above the lower one. *The Grand Scribe's Records* state that flagpoles 10 metres high were ranged along the lower storey and both accounts state that 10,000 people could be entertained in the great hall on the upper storey.[24] Archaeological excavations show that the area enclosed was closer to the larger estimate and that there was a rammed-earth platform 8 metres high at the back of the enclosure, so the raised terraces of the front, the more significant part of the complex, could have been significantly higher.

The figure of 10,000 guests is probably not numerically accurate for the number 10,000 was widely used in traditional China to suggest a lot of things, 'a myriad', rather than an accurate head count. It remains a unit of measurement in China today: if you tell a Chinese person that your house is worth £200,000, for example, you would actually say that it is worth 20 *wan* or 20 times 10,000. The use of 10,000, together with the alleged dimensions of the hall, provoke a slightly exasperated response and a call for a return to reason in the Qin–Han volume in the *Cambridge History of China*, where it is noted that the much smaller throne room of AD 60–65 (86 × 16 metres) was also described as being able comfortably to contain 10,000 visitors and that the massive central hall in the Forbidden City, whose capacity has not been set down, is a mere 60 × 30 metres.[25] But it seems from the size and scale revealed in the excavation of the First Emperor's Hipped Roof Hall that, even if the number of guests might have been exaggerated, the size of the hall was not. If the entire palace, of which the Hipped Roof Hall was merely a part, had been completed and renamed, its extent would surely have been quite extraordinary.

Another widely quoted figure associated with the Hipped Roof Hall was that of 700,000 labourers, including criminals and those on labour service, who were said to have been drafted in to work on both the hall and the First Emperor's tomb, which was also started in 212 BC.[26] As a statistic it is rather more credible than the alleged 10,000 guests that the hall was supposed to accommodate. For as well as including workers on both sites, it possibly includes those who worked in the kilns that produced the enormous quantity of bricks and tiles found. These include impressed floor tiles with patterns of whorls, animals, sunflowers, leaves and inscriptions. One such inscription, stating that 'The whole empire is filled with subjects, the annual harvest has all ripened, may no person go hungry on the streets', is reminiscent of the triumphal inscriptions that the First Emperor set up all over his empire.[27] Here he could tread upon a reminder of his glory in the first hall in his massive palace.

When the First Emperor's dynasty was overthrown in 210 BC, the hall is said to have burned for five days, which is perhaps another indication of its immense size.

IO

The Drugs of Immortality

Much debate about the First Emperor has revolved around systems of thought, and particularly around the differences between Confucianism and Legalism, and it has been pointed out that these systems of thought are 'this-worldly', concerned with man's place in society and without much reference to death and none at all to the avoidance of death.[1] Yet it is clear from the attention paid to grave goods and the increasing complexity of provisions for the dead from the Neolithic period through to the time of the First Emperor, that though they were not part of the intellectual systems of the time, beliefs about death and the afterlife were highly developed.

From the account of the First Emperor's life in *The Grand Scribe's Records*, it appears that after having settled the pattern of his rule, he became increasingly interested in the possibilities of immortality. He visited many sacred mountains, places close to heaven, where he made significant sacrifices. In 219 BC, after he had made sacrifices and set up an inscribed stone stele on Mount Langya, he met some men who might be described as practitioners of the occult arts or 'recipe gentlemen'.[2] Some have called them 'necromancers', magicians who claimed to be able to communicate with the dead. Though necromancy may be an acceptable English term, 'recipe gentlemen' is a more straightforward translation of the Chinese and a better description of their activities, for they were above all concerned with herbs and potions designed to extend life and not with contacting the dead.

The recipe gentlemen presented a memorial to the First Emperor: 'In the ocean are three fairy islands ... where immortals live. We beg to be sent in search of these with some young girls and boys after fasting and purification.'[3] The First Emperor sent the recipe gentlemen off with several thousand young boys and girls, perhaps attractive to immortals because of their innocence and purity, to sail the East China Sea in search of the islands of immortality.

A further three recipe gentlemen were sent off to search for the herbs of immortality four years later, in 215 BC. The first contingent of thousands of young girls and boys was never seen again but of the second group, one returned, empty-handed and reporting difficulties. He is said to have complained to another scholar that the First Emperor was obsessed with power, spending hours every night reading bamboo-slip reports, and that this obsession meant it was impossible to find an elixir of long life for him.

Despite the banning and burning of the books in 213 BC, the First Emperor had continued to complain about the conspiracies of scholars, but it was the failure of the recipe men that really enraged him. 'I collected all the writings of the empire and got rid of those which were no use. I assembled a host of scholars and alchemists to start a reign of peace, hoping the alchemists would find marvellous herbs. But I am told no more has been heard of the [first recipe gentleman] and those who went with him while the [second recipe gentleman]'s crowd has wasted millions without obtaining any elixir – all I hear from them is charges of corruption.'[4]

Subsequently, the First Emperor, 'unable to find happiness, ordered the court scholars to write poems about immortals and pure beings, and wherever he went he made court musicians set these to music and sing them'.[5] In 210 BC, he set off on what was to be his last journey, to the coast to look over the East China Sea where the isles of the immortals were said to be. He reflected on the fact that the second recipe gentleman had reported that the herbs of immortality on the islands were guarded by fierce whales but that he did not have the means to kill them. Repeating crossbows seemed to be the answer. The First Emperor dreamt that a sea god came to him and recommended sacrifices. These were carried out and then the First Emperor ordered crossbows and eventually shot some large fish himself. Within a short time, he was dead.

Ideas about immortality current at the time varied but they were all based on beliefs about the body and the soul. It was thought that two spiritual elements were associated with the body. One, called *po*, was the life force that kept the body active, while the other, *hun*, was the expressive, emotional soul. It was generally believed that the body and its two spiritual elements separated at death, with the *hun* going off to paradise or, if unlucky, to the gloomy Yellow Springs, a place thought of as not as bad as hell, and certainly not as hot, rather a dark, damp, dismal realm. Providing that the burial arrangements were satisfactory, the *po* would stay with the body and cause no harm. However, if a person had suffered or, as in the case of General Meng, had died far from home without a proper burial, a ghost spirit might emerge, capable of returning to earth to haunt people and cause harm.[6]

The 'this-worldly' view characteristic of early Chinese philosophy led to a great stress on longevity. Bronzes inscribed with prayers for blessing most commonly called for longevity. Various related terms show that from the eighth century BC, there were thought to be different aspects to longevity. Some, such as 'preservation of the body', reflected the view that if the body was preserved from decay after death, this conferred a form of immortality. This derived from the idea that, after death, the spirit only lasted as long as the body, dying when it decayed. The desire to preserve the body and keep the *po* spirit alive led to burial customs seen in the Han dynasty when jade, believed to protect the corpse from physical decay, was widely used to plug the body's orifices and, in the most extreme example, to create body suits, like armour made from square plaques of green jade, which clothed the entire body.[7]

Another form of immortality was expressed as 'transcending the world' or 'ascending to the distant place'.[8] By this means, the person effectively left the world to live as an immortal. References to such immortals seem to date back to the early fourth century BC, one being described as having 'flesh and skin ... like ice and snow. He did not eat ... but inhaled the wind and drank the dew. He rode on clouds, drove along the flying dragons and thus rambled beyond the four seas.'[9] Such other-worldly characters eventually assumed a prime place in Chinese mythology as the 'Eight Immortals'. Stories of their ascent into the heavens included one floating on a leaf, another borne aloft on a celestial stork and yet another who travelled on his magic sword, using it like a skateboard. A fourth rode thousands of miles a day on a white mule and when the journey was over, he would fold the mule up like a piece of paper and put it in his pocket. If these Immortals ate, and many did not, it was only powdered mother-of-pearl, miracle pills or the peaches of immortality, and they drank magic potions and much wine.[10]

It seems that the First Emperor did not seek this form of immortality but rather a method of extending his physical life on earth. By avoiding death, the body, the *po* and the *hun* would remain intact and not be separated. Keeping the body alive forever was said to be achievable through ingesting elixirs sometimes made up of mineral components such as gold and pearls, mentioned in the *Discourses on Salt and Iron* of the first century BC.[11] During the First Emperor's lifetime it was believed that the immortals who lived on islands in the East China Sea cultivated herbs, particularly the 'herb of death-lessness' (a mushroom), which could confer immortality. It was for this reason that the thousands of young boys and girls were sent off to search for the fabled islands. It was also, presumably, in these fabled (but non-existent, unless they meant Japan) islands that the second group of recipe gentlemen were thwarted by savage whales.

It is nowhere recorded which drugs, whether plant or mineral, the First Emperor may have ingested in his quest for immortality, although it has been suggested that he took pills made from a distinctly poisonous mixture of gold, mercury, jade, sulphur, cinnabar, orpiment, quartz and lead, 'dissolved' in a herbal mixture.[12] It was, apparently, the incorruptible nature of these minerals that was transferred to the body. Later literature records an enormous variety of plants, the 'herbs of deathlessness', which supposedly possessed this same quality and which may well have been used earlier on too. They include mushrooms and fungi, ferns, tree fruits such as pine nuts, onions and garlic, asparagus, lilies, ginger, lotuses, white-flowered peonies, magnolia, bamboo, *Rosa banksiae*, cassia, sophora, citrus, ginger, ginseng and chrysanthemum as well as about a hundred others.

It is interesting that a number of fungi and parasitic plants are

28. The fungus of immortality, nineteenth century

listed, perhaps because of their opportunistic lifestyle and ability to grow from a dead host. One author reported that during the time of the First Emperor, a 'herb of deathlessness' was discovered. 'When the bodies of many men unrighteously and untimely killed, were lying about Ferghana ... birds resembling crows or ravens appeared carrying this plant in their bills and placed it on the faces of those corpses, so that they immediately sat up and were restored to life.'[13] The Emperor had a sample of the herb sent to a specialist who reported that it was 'the herb of deathlessness', also known as 'the mushroom that nourishes the spirit', that its leaves looked like the leaves of the water-grass and that one stalk was enough to raise the dead. No one knows what it was, but the recipe gentleman said that it grew 'among the roseate rocks' of an island in the eastern sea, hence the imperially commissioned sea trips to search for it.

Conifers such as pine and thuja were chosen for their own longevity and the positive symbolism of their evergreen foliage. The resin was used, and one sage who ate nothing but pine kernels

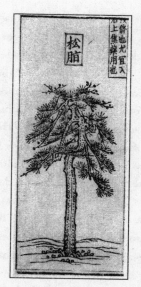

29. *The source of pine nuts, a source of longevity*

grew hairs 'seven digits long' all over his body, and his eyes took on a square shape. When he walked it was as if he was transported by the winds, and he could overtake galloping horses. Though he sent some pine kernels to the (mythical) Emperor Yao, who allegedly reigned from 2357 to 2256 BC, and though the Emperor is said to have been too busy to eat them, the length of his supposed reign suggests considerable natural longevity.[14]

In the popular imagination, the First Emperor was terrified of death, though he survived three assassination attempts, and he became increasingly superstitious in his search for immortality. In his modern novel, *Le Grand Empereur et ses automates* (1985), Jean Levi depicts him as following Daoist sexual rituals, surrounding himself with incense made from resin, myrrh and cardamom, hallucinating from eating pills made from realgar and suffering from terrible headaches and stomach problems.[15] He complains to one of his recipe gentlemen, 'Meditation bores me and the contemplation of my viscera makes me feel sick. My insides are ravaged by mineral drugs and pills made of resin, orpiment, cinnabar and mica. My body is on fire. Since I gave up eating grain and chose only dried meat and jujubes instead of juicy roast meat, I have had terrible stomach pains. Breathing exercises make me dizzy and give me ringing in the ears. And despite my diet, my bowels don't function. I need something else!'[16]

According to *The Grand Scribe's Records*, the recipe gentlemen complained that it was the First Emperor's devotion to work, rather than alchemical excess, which made it difficult for him to achieve immortality. Rather than one obsessed with chemical escape, he might have been, like some of the best of the later emperors, excessively concerned with the minutiae of government. According to one story that has been ignored ever since, he would not sleep until he had read a daily quota of 30 kilos of official documents.[17]

Seas of Mercury, Pearl Stars and an Army of 8,000 Men

Though contemporaries, including the First Emperor himself, were far more concerned with beliefs that centred on death and burial and the survival of the plural souls, as has been noted in the previous chapter, subsequent discussion about the belief systems before and during his reign has generally focused on the moral and political issues in the debate between Confucianism and Legalism.

Legalism was concerned with the behaviour of live citizens, not their souls. Confucianism, too, was above all this-worldly. In the *Judgements and Conversations* or collection of Confucius' sayings, there are hardly more than five references to death and they are all set in the context of the bereaved, not the dead. Two references stress the importance of sincerity in ritual: 'He sacrificed to the dead as if they were present. He sacrificed to the spirits as if the spirits were present,' and, 'In ceremonies of mourning, it is better there be deep sorrow than a minute attention to observances.'[1] Observance of the proprieties was important to Confucius who would 'not eat to the full' if he was eating beside someone in mourning. Nor would he

30. Preparing a sacrifice

sing on a day he had attended a burial.[2] In another passage, he talked of filiality in terms of a man's behaviour before and after his father's death, when performance of the proper rituals and, above all, adherence to the father's actions and beliefs were deemed praiseworthy.[3] Finally, he noted that 'The superior man dislikes the thought of his name not being mentioned after his death.' As far as Confucius was concerned, reputation and memory were clearly more significant than the physical preservation of the corpse or the whereabouts of the two souls.

That is not to say that ordinary Confucian believers did not carry out elaborate rituals at a time of bereavement. One critic of the fourth century BC noted that 'when a parent dies, the Confucians lay out the corpse for a long time before dressing it for burial. They climb on the roof, peer down the well, poke in the rat holes and search in the wash basins, looking for the soul of the dead man.'[4]

Where Confucianism officially concentrated on the importance of carrying out the correct rituals properly, the other main strand of philosophical thought, Daoism, offered no alternative consolation. One of the major Daoist works stressed the normality of death as part of the endless cycle of nature, diminishing the significance of Confucian ritual but promoting an attitude of acceptance. The philosopher Zhuangzi is said to have attended the funeral of the other great Daoist philosopher, Laozi (who may never have existed[5]), and against all propriety and ritual, uttered three yells and left. He explained that weeping at a funeral was a 'crime of violating the principle of nature'. 'The master came because it was his natural time; he went because it was his natural course. Those who abide by their time and follow their natural course cannot be affected by sorrow or joy … Things are born and die without holding to any permanence.'[6] True to his philosophy, as has been noted, when his own wife died, Zhuangzi was found cheerfully drumming on an upturned bowl. He explained that she was merely sleeping in the Great Inner Room.[7]

Though 'philosophical Daoism' offered no view of the afterlife, cheering or otherwise, the recipe gentlemen whom the First Emperor consulted in such numbers in his search for physical longevity and consequent immortality are often associated with Daoism. Even so, it is probable that they developed their ideas and recipes independently of any school of thought in a straightforward response to the eternal human fear of death and extinction.[8] Funeral and burial practices in ancient China developed out of that fear rather than from any complex philosophical reasoning. They also developed well before the time of Confucius (c. 551–479 BC) and persisted well after.

正面

商瑚文
漢陽葉東鄉藏

文二字在瑚之末
精古欵識稱科學術
釋為瑚字

31. A decorated bronze halberd

According to *The Grand Scribe's Records*, human sacrifice at burials only began in 678 BC when one of the First Emperor's ancestors was laid in his tomb and 'for the first time, human victims were made to follow a dead person into the grave'.[9] In fact, the nobility of the Shang dynasty (c. 1600–1045 BC) were interred in deep underground pits, their coffins surrounded by bronzes, axes, pottery, jade, cowrie shells (then used as money) and skeletons. In one pit, 48 humans and 6 dogs have been found, in another 20 skeletons, 2 isolated skulls and 12 dogs. Sometimes chariots were buried, together with the horses that drew them.[10] In the subsequent Western Zhou period (1045–771 BC), aristocrats were buried with the 'paraphernalia' that enabled them to perform the two chief duties owed to the state, waging war and making sacrifices, so ritual bronzes used to make offerings to gods and ancestors, as well as chariots for warfare, were included in the grave.[11]

By the mid-Eastern Zhou period, around the sixth century BC, except in the largest aristocratic tombs, a complete assemblage of ritual bronzes, precious objects and war chariots was no longer found. Instead they were gradually replaced by 'spirit utensils', miniature versions of the real things, often made in cheaper materials such as straw, wood or ceramics. In the *Spring and Autumn Annals*, a chronology of events from 722 to 481 BC traditionally included in the Confucian Classics, there is a note that says that it is more 'filial' to include these smaller, cheaper 'spirit utensils' since the tomb is then less likely to be looted – for looting would leave the dead 'destitute for all eternity'.[12]

It is clear from the inclusion of real and, eventually, miniaturized objects of the sort used in daily life, that there was a strong popular belief that the deceased needed to carry on after death as in life. If the *hun* soul left for paradise soon after death, the *po* spirit that remained with the body after death, and perhaps the body itself, needed implements in order to carry on, to remain happy and not turn into a vengeful ghost, causing harm and unhappiness to those left behind. As time passed, the idea of provisions for the dead grew beyond the supply of bronzes for sacrifice and chariots for war. In the tomb of an aristocratic woman buried near Changsha in 168 BC, containers have been found holding two kinds of beer, rice, wheat, barley, millet, soybeans and red lentils as well as beef and rice stew, dog meat and celery stew, venison, fish, soy sauce, sugar, honey and salted beans. She was also buried with her walking stick and miniature figurines made from lacquered wood of dancers and musicians to entertain her.[13]

A story of resurrection in the early Qin may have influenced grave provision. A man named Dan killed himself in 297 BC but was released again from his tomb three years later, after much digging by a numinous white dog. It seems that he was not really meant to die at that time and it was the 'result of faulty record-keeping by the netherworld bureaucracy' which was subsequently rectified. When he reappeared, Dan reported that the dead did not need much clothing but he was specific about the food arrangements. After food sacrifices were offered, careful washing-up was necessary, and he insisted that hot water should not be poured over food offerings or the ghosts would not eat it and would go hungry.[14]

Developments in the form of the tomb itself also occurred. The tomb of a marquis buried at Leigudun in 433 BC included twenty-two human sacrifices and a dog, a full set of musical instruments in the form of bronze bells and jade chimes, furniture, food vessels, many bronze weapons and a couple of chariots.[15] The tomb itself was divided into four chambers set in a deep vertical pit. It is thought that these represented the four parts of the marquis's palace: his living quarters (the tomb chamber), the ceremonial area, the arsenal and the harem, all filled with appropriate grave goods.

The First Emperor, with all these ideas in mind, ordered work to start on the building of his tomb as soon as he took control of the empire. There seems to have been an extra push in 212 BC, when 700,000 convicts and forced labourers were sent to work both on his proposed new palace and the tomb. The tomb proper is a rammed-earth, four-sided pyramid with three stepped levels, a massive artificial hill lying between the Wei River and Mount Li, 35 kilometres east of the First Emperor's capital. It once stood 120 metres high but time has eroded it and it is now only 64 metres above ground level. The mound was built in the southern end of a double-walled compound. The outer wall, over 6 kilometres long, represents a city wall, and the inner wall, that around a palace compound, placed towards the south, just as the great palace lay south of the capital. Inside the city wall, to the north, building foundations have been unearthed as well as the remains of stables, store-houses and sacrificial altars or temples.

The tomb mound itself has not yet been excavated, partly because the detailed description of its contents in *The Grand Scribe's Records* has rather intimidated archaeologists. They fear that the tomb was desecrated in 206 BC by the invading Han army and that current techniques would not be able to save the contents when exposed to the air. *The Grand Scribe's Records* describes how the tomb was built. 'They dug through three strata of streams, poured in liquid bronze, and secured the sarcophagus. Terracotta houses, officials, unusual and valuable things were moved in to fill it. He [the First Emperor] ordered artisans to make crossbows triggered by mechanisms. Anyone passing before them would be shot immediately. They used mercury to create rivers, the [Yangtze] and the [Yellow River], and the great seas, wherein the mercury was circulated mechanically. On the ceiling were the celestial bodies and on the ground geographical features. The candles were made of oil of dugong, which was not supposed to burn out for a long time.'

The First Emperor's son declared that all concubines who had no sons should be buried with the First Emperor, and when it was pointed out that the workmen who had built the tomb knew all about its contents, they too were buried alive when the tomb was closed up.[16] Burials of rich individuals with grave goods including jade, gold and silver have been found outside the necropolis's outer walls, and other mass burials of over a hundred workers involved in construction have been discovered to the west.[17] The only tentative efforts to explore the tomb have been magnetic scans, revealing the presence of a large number of coins, leading to the hope that the treasury was interred with the First Emperor, though it is unlikely that the Second Emperor, who was involved in the closing of the tomb and the massacre of concubines and artisans, would have permitted this. Scans of the soil on top of the mound have revealed an unusually high concentration of mercury, supposedly in the form of China's waterways. It seems odd that mercury should rise but perhaps the loss of the top of the mound over two millennia has meant that the tomb chamber is now nearer the surface.

The mound and its surrounding walls and buildings clearly express two beliefs. The first was that the First Emperor was a cosmic ruler, in touch with the heavens and the earth in the broadest sense; the second was that he was also an earthly ruler who would continue to preside over the capital as represented in the walls built around the mound and the incorporation of stables (for warring chariots and horses) and temples or altars for sacrifice. The removal of significant shrines to the necropolis served to underline the First Emperor's continuing presence since sacrifices continued to be offered there four times a day.[18]

The tomb also incorporates the notion that the ruler's tasks, on earth and beyond, were to observe ritual and wage war. More recently it has been seen as a 'living environment modelled on the mundane world', a 'fictive' but 'efficacious reality' with the inclusion of practical, earthly objects, which enabled the spirit and body to continue in death as in life. Three hundred horses, accompanied by terracotta grooms, were buried in the stables and real straw was found there too.[19]

The tomb mound has always been known as such, for it has stood above ground ever since it was erected in 210 BC. A half life-size clay figure of a seated woman, found near the tumulus, was exhibited in London in 1973. She kneels, her hands resting in her lap, dressed in a long cross-over gown, with her hair pulled back in a complex bun at the back of her head. The caption in the catalogue accompanying the exhibition does not reveal exactly when she was found although it does mention a similar figure discovered nearby in 1932.[20] However, it was not until 1974 that further discoveries were made which indicated that the mound was only part of a massive complex whose full extent still remains unknown.

In that year, local peasants digging a well uncovered the first of the pits containing the Buried Army. In all four pits have been found, although the fourth was empty. From the other three, around 8,000 life-size pottery warriors have been uncovered. The excitement of the find is hard to describe. When I took a group of tourists there in about 1978, the main pit was still open to the sky and archaeologists were working in a series of tents set up on site. When he discovered that I knew Chinese, the archaeologist who had been told to show us around seized my hand and dragged me at top speed to his favourite spots, unwilling to wait patiently whilst the interpreter slowly translated his explanation. We ran along the trench as he pointed out different faces, different attitudes, different soldiers, and I tried to shout back to the group what he was saying. This was his work, and had been his work for several years, but the thrill of discovery was still alive. The scale of this main pit alone is also its greatest significance. It measures about 210 metres by 60 metres, with eleven parallel corridors containing 3,210 life-size or slightly larger than life-size warrior figures.[21] As we ran along the top, it was clear, even at speed, that the figures varied greatly in their armour, hairstyles and stances.

Facing east, towards the imperial tumulus, the army in Pit 1 comprised a varied formation. There is a vanguard unit of bowmen and crossbowmen, with outer files of archers, and behind them stand thirty-six files of foot soldiers in armour, originally carrying spears or swords. Behind them in turn is a pottery squad of six chariots and more infantry squads with a rearguard of armoured infantrymen.[22] In Pit 2, around 1,400 ceramic cavalrymen and charioteers were discovered, with accompanying bowmen, both kneeling and standing, and infantrymen. The third pit, northwest of Pit 1, contained only 68 figures, including a number of 'officer' figures, and it has been interpreted as a command post. It is assumed that the fourth, empty pit was unfinished when the First Emperor died.[23]

All the pits contained partition walls lined with timbers that supported a light roof structure. The bottom of the corridors in which the terracotta soldiers stood were covered with bricks. The roof structure was of horizontal timbers covered with matting and a couple of metres of earth. In Pits 1 and 2 there is clear evidence of fire, deliberately set by the invading Han armies before they moved on to burn the capital.

It has been assumed that owing to the asymmetrical arrangement of the armies, there might have been parallel pits on the east side of the tomb mound, but probes have not yet revealed their existence. Nevertheless, other burials have continued to be found. Two half life-size bronze chariots were discovered in 1980, a group of thick-set, muscular acrobats soon after, and a crowd of wetland birds cast in bronze in 2005.

The ceramic figures of soldiers, cavalrymen and charioteers, as well as the ceramic horses, are an extraordinary example of factory production. Though the kilns in which they were made have not yet been discovered, some of the stamped ceramic floor tiles of the palace in the capital and the ceramic figures for the tomb have the same names incised on them, indicating that skilled ceramic workers moved from one site to the other.[24] There may also have been movement of slightly less skilled ceramic workers. The great palace hall was drained by ceramic pipes, while the legs of the ceramic soldiers, which are largely undifferentiated, bear more than a passing resemblance to drain-pipes.

Most of the soldier figures from the Buried Army consist of seven separate parts, each separately moulded and then joined together. These were the moulded plinth on which they stood or knelt, moulded arms, legs, feet, hands, head and torso. These basic parts were standardized in different moulds, with two-part moulds for the head, for example. Once the basic parts were assembled, a variety of details were added. Hats, hairstyles, eyebrows and moustaches were individually modelled and ears (formed in moulds) attached along the join of the two halves of the head moulds. Though there is an apparent distinction between many of the figures, archaeologists have discovered only 'three types of plinth, two types of feet, three types of shoes and four types of boots, two types of legs, eight types of torso, and two types of armour, each category having three subtypes'. The most varied parts are the heads, showing eight different types.[25] Though this sounds quite standardized, as anyone who has seen the Buried Army will remember, the effect is of extraordinary variety, and it is fascinating to learn that this has been achieved through varying a limited number of possibilities. The suggestion that the figures represent portraits cannot be upheld, for quite apart from the practical difficulties involved in gathering together thousands of soldiers for ceramic artisans to take their likeness in clay, the assembly of the Buried Army was an industrial rather than an artistic project. As Lothar Ledderose points out, there were only two types of hand forms found amongst the 16,000 hands of the terracotta warriors, yet their use, their precise placing in the long sleeves of gown or tunic and the angles used, helped create an illusion of individuality.[26] It is the most extraordinary example of creative mass-production in the world.

Looking at the detail of mass-production followed by hand finishing, various features stand out. The soles of the shoes of the kneeling archers, modelled over 2,000 years ago, are exactly the same as the home-made shoes worn by many Chinese even in the late 1970s. Such shoes were stitched at home, and the thick cotton thread drawn through the white cotton shoe sole formed a sort of tread or grip.[27] Others have remarked upon the extraordinary variety of hairstyles. Men at the time wore their hair long, but tied up, usually in a bun on the top of the head and definitely favouring one side or the other. Such hairstyles persisted until 1644 when the Manchu Qing dynasty imposed the long plait or queue (on pain of death) on all Chinese men, but even in the late 1970s it was still possible to find ancient Daoist priests in Sichuan province wearing the pre-Qing bun hairstyle. Hairstyles on the soldiers of the Buried Army reveal various approaches to the bun, with plaits criss-crossing the head and ending up in the bun. Threads tying the plaits were coloured bright red, as were the threads holding the armour plaques together.[28]

Perched on top of the complex weaving of plaits and buns are a stunning variety of hats. There are simple stockinette caps pulled to one side or the other by the angle of the bun or practical, flattish, ear-flapped caps for the ordinary soldiers, and complicated folded and stiffened satin curls and whorls and little lacquer boxes perched on the heads of generals.[29] All, whether generals with soft silk scarves tied in a variety of styles around their necks to stop their armour chafing, or officials with pie-frilled collars, wear cross-over knee-length gowns with trousers/leggings and boots or shoes. An under-tunic, also cross-over in style, is often visible at the neck. This fairly practical costume, the short gown and leggings allowing freedom of movement, is a reminder that long ago, in the fourth century BC, a Warring States ruler had suggested opting for 'barbarian' clothing, or short tunics and trousers, as more suited to effective cavalry work and therefore more efficient in battle.[30] Many of the figures wear armour in the form of leather or lacquer scales riveted together or attached by leather strips, and mostly in the form of jerkins or waistcoats.[31] The pieces of armour were also mass-moulded but then applied individually.

One aspect of the figures that is not immediately apparent to the visitor is the fact that all the warriors originally carried real weapons, bronze spears and swords, and though 10,000 have been found, this represents a fraction of the original number, most apparently carried off as useful weapons by the invading Han army which looted the tumulus and set fire to the pits containing the Buried Army in 206 BC.[32] The weapons included bows and arrows, and formidable cross-bows with a bronze mechanism. There were also bronze lances, daggers, axes and various types of knives, all originally fitted on wooden or bamboo handles. A weapon of particular interest was a sword, 90 centimetres long and found to be quite without rust despite 2,000 years underground. It was as strong as steel and its condition was said to be the result of the treatment of the surface, 'oxidized with chromium'.[33]

Another feature of the original army was that the figures and horses were also coloured, though virtually none of the pigment now remains. Firing the figures, which were of thick clay, must have been a complicated business, for there is the risk of collapse in firing thick clay or clay of varying thickness. It is presumed that they were coloured after firing, with a coating of lacquer applied first and then mineral-based pigments. This probably also took place near the tumulus, although the workshops have still not been discovered. Some infantrymen wore green robes with lavender-patterned collar and cuffs and black shoes with red laces. Others had short coats in red with blue collar and cuffs, and many had blue trousers. The ceramic horses were painted brown and black with white hoofs and teeth, and red paint was used inside the ears, nostrils and mouth.[34]

Other pits discovered near the outer wall of the tomb complex include one containing 'rare animals', particularly different deer including muntjac, their skeletons accompanied, like the horses in the stables, by half life-size kneeling ceramic attendants, and also one containing 'stone armour', suits made of stone squares pierced with holes in imitation of the leather and lacquer squares used at the time for armour and seen on many of the ceramic figures in the Buried Army. No real soldier of the time could have worn stone armour as he would not have been able to move. The suits, made up from 612 pieces of stone joined with bronze wire, weigh 20 kilos each. Perhaps such suits were fundamentally symbolic armour.[35]

Another nearby pit contained the sort of entertainers seen in the tomb of the aristocratic lady from Changsha, in this case, twelve solid, muscular, life-size ceramic acrobats, with bare torsos and short

32. Acrobats from a Han dynasty tomb brick

skirts, ready to tumble, lift weights and juggle for the posthumous pleasure of the First Emperor. They are barefoot, some apparently carrying their shoes, and their legs are skilfully and accurately modelled, unlike those of the soldiers. They were found together with a massive bronze tripod of a sort usually used in ritual sacrifice but here thought to be something used by the jugglers and acrobats in their routine.[36] A more recent discovery has been the model 'wetland' with life-size bronze geese and swans.

The two half life-size bronze chariots unearthed in 1980 were of different types, though both were harnessed to four bronze horses hitched side by side. Each was made up of over 3,000 separate bronze pieces, including tiny parts for the bridles, bits and reins, and each weighs over 1,000 kilos. In addition they were decorated with about 7 kilos of silver and gold. One chariot was open, though a bronze parasol, complete with ribs, was set behind the driver who stood at the front of the chariot with a bronze bow, arrows and quiver beside him. The other chariot was the sort in which it is thought the First Emperor travelled when on his journeys through China and is sometimes described as a sleeping chariot. It is easy to see how the First

33. 'Wetland' wildfowl

Emperor's death could have been concealed by placing the body in such an enclosed chariot. Behind the driver's seat (he sits on his heels as he holds the reins) is a low, rectangular construction with a similar, parasol-like roof. The bronze is modelled to suggest that the real thing would have been made of bamboo, wood and leather, and covered with swirling cloud patterns in silver and gold. There is a door at the rear and, on either side, bronze lattice windows which can be opened and shut.[37]

Though it is clear from continuing discoveries that the full extent of the First Emperor's tomb complex is still unknown, and that it appears to have been unfinished at the time of his death, we will probably never know on what scale it had been planned. Looked at in the context of earlier and later burial practices, it seems to mark a significant turning-point. Earlier royal burials often included human and animal sacrifices: so did the First Emperor's tomb. Later imperial burials tended to include miniature ceramic models of people, animals, buildings and ritual vessels, and half-sized chariots, ceramic serving women and stable attendants: so did the First Emperor's. His Buried Army of life-size or larger-than-life soldiers, with their real weapons, is unique, however.

The presentation of the First Emperor as an earthly ruler, with his 'city-palace' tomb which included a recreation of the world with its mercury rivers and seas, was paralleled by the presentation of him as controller of the cosmos with the heavenly constellations picked out in pearls on the ceiling of his tomb chamber. The tomb's mixture of the real (straw for horse skeletons, bronze geese, ceramic acrobats and soldiers) and the less than real (half-size servants and half-size chariots), together with a real representation of the imperial army in life-size clay models, suggests a gradual movement towards an understanding that the real world did not have to be present but that it could be represented in the grave.[38]

It would be fascinating to know what the First Emperor's contribution to the creation of his immense mausoleum was, if any. As a man obsessed by an apparent fear of death, taking every opportunity to find people or potions that would ensure bodily immortality, he may have left all the details to others or he may have directed much of the activity, but there is no record of his involvement either way.

12

The First Emperor and the Great Helmsman

For 2,000 years, the First Emperor remained condemned by Confucian orthodoxy for his failure to rule 'with humanity and righteousness', as one critic put it in his essay 'The Faults of Qin', written less than a century after the First Emperor's death. As the legend of his brutal burying of scholars was exaggerated, so, too, legends like that of the faithful wife of Meng, weeping for her husband who died hundreds of miles from home on the First Emperor's Great Wall, gradually added to the picture of a cruel despot with no mitigating features. One scholar of the Tang dynasty, Liu Zongyuan (AD 773–819), who lived at a time when China's stability was threatened by internal rebellion and external threats from the barbarians beyond the borders, wrote a rare essay praising the Qin bureaucracy which remained loyal and stable in difficult circumstances. Nearly a thousand years later, another scholar, writing in the mid-seventeenth century as the Chinese Ming dynasty fell to the invading Manchu armies, praised the imperial bureaucracy established by the First Emperor as the best response to China's needs.[1]

Such rare instances apart, it was not until 1973 that the First Emperor was finally reassessed and some of his ideas and achievements widely praised. The reassessment took place against the unusual background of a fierce, and finally fatal, power struggle between Chairman Mao, the Great Helmsman, and Lin Biao, his designated successor and 'close comrade-in-arms'.

During the early period of Communist rule, and amongst Communist scholars even before 1949, the First Emperor was still generally regarded as a tyrant. In 1943, Guo Moruo (1892–1978), poet, playwright, historian, epigrapher and politician, President of the Chinese Academy of Sciences and the major cultural figure at the top of the Chinese Communist Party, wrote an article on the First Emperor which concluded that he achieved power largely through luck and that he had made the mistake of casting aside the Prime Minister, who had been a restraining force, in favour of the tougher Councillor.

A pretentious polymath, Guo Moruo developed a portrait of the First Emperor based on medical and psychoanalytic theories which seem to have had little basis in any real evidence. No portraits or even real physical descriptions of the First Emperor exist but Guo Moruo insisted, probably on the basis of a description in *The Grand Scribe's Records*, that he was 'physically deformed, with a protruding chest, a saddle-like nose and an unpleasant voice'. Furthermore, he was 'psychologically disturbed and abnormal' because of his mother's relationship with her eunuch 'lover'. Guo Moruo also diagnosed him as suffering from bronchial problems and cartilage disease.[2]

Before 1973, Chairman Mao made several ambivalent statements about the First Emperor. In a poem, 'Snow', written in 1936, after marvelling at the glory of snow on the landscape, he turned rather suddenly to the great rulers of the past and regretted that the First Emperor, amongst others, was 'lacking in literary grace'.[3]

North country scene
A hundred leagues locked in ice
A thousand leagues of whirling snow.
Both sides of the Great Wall
One single white immensity.
The Yellow River's swift current
Is stilled from end to end.
The mountains dance like silver snakes
And the highlands change like wax-hued elephants
Vying with heaven in stature.
On a fine day, the land
Clad in white, adorned in red,
Grows more enchanting.

This land so rich in beauty
Has made countless heroes bow in homage.
But alas! The First Emperor and Han Wudi
Were lacking in literary grace.
And Tang Taizong and Song Taizu
Had little poetry in their souls;
And Genghis Khan,
Son of Heaven for a day,
Knew only shooting eagles, bow outstretched.
All are past and gone!
For truly great men
Look to this age alone.[4]

There is no real evidence that the First Emperor lacked literary brilliance, for the only surviving writings in which he might have had a hand are the stone stelae recording his political and administrative achievements. Indeed the First Emperor's travels to famous mountains and scenic spots in China might suggest that he was, in fact, quite sensitive to natural beauty, even if he never took up his brush to record his impressions. And a close reading of the poem, where the disparaging introduction of these rulers of the past is something of a non sequitur, suggests that only the writer, seeing himself as a great ruler also capable of writing sensitive poetry, is truly, historically great.

In 1958, a year after a campaign which had resulted in 300,000 intellectuals being branded 'rightists', effectively ending their careers as writers or teachers, Chairman Mao made a further pronouncement on the First Emperor.[5] The 1957 call to 'let a hundred flowers bloom and a hundred schools of thought contend', probably launched by Chairman Mao in response to Khrushchev's denunciation of Stalin and the cult of the personality and the Hungarian uprising of 1956, was interpreted by China's intellectuals as a chance to air their grievances against the Chinese Communist Party. The tragic result of their speaking out was the 'Campaign against Rightists' which was enacted only a few months later, removing them from their jobs and often banishing them to the remote countryside for decades or even for life.

In May 1958, with the intellectuals satisfactorily silenced, Mao boasted of how he had outdone the First Emperor: 'He buried 460 scholars alive; we have buried 460,000 scholars … we have surpassed the [First Emperor] a hundredfold.'[6] In the same speech, Mao is reported to have praised the First Emperor for his refusal to follow tradition slavishly and his emphasis on the needs of the present rather than harking back to a mythical golden age. He said that the First Emperor was 'an authority in emphasizing the present whilst slighting the past' and quoted him as saying that 'Those who use the past to criticize the present should have their clans exterminated.'[7] According to some sources, Mao's boast about having gone further and done better than the First Emperor was made in response to an interruption by Lin Biao, a leading general, soon to be made Minister of National Defence and named as Chairman Mao's successor.[8]

In mid-September 1971, Lin Biao and his wife and son died in a plane crash in Mongolia. The circumstances of the flight and crash remain mysterious. Since 1966, when Chairman Mao launched the Great Proletarian Cultural Revolution to purge the Chinese Communist Party of corruption and transform 'culture', China had been in a state of turmoil, approaching civil war. 'Culture' and 'cultural revolution' have to be understood in the Marxist context. Marxist economic historians divided the economy, the infrastructure or the base, from the superstructure of national institutions: government, politics, the administration, education and, in the sense we understand it, culture.

By the early 1960s, Mao felt that the economy had been successfully transformed into a socialist economy but that the rest, the cultural superstructure, had not been transformed. Those at the top, particularly in the Chinese Communist Party, had become complacent and corrupt to the point where Mao said in 1964, 'At present, you can buy a Party Branch Secretary for a few packs of cigarettes, not to mention marrying a daughter to him.'[9] This view was developed against the background of the Sino-Soviet split of 1961 and the continuing rivalry between China and the Soviet Union for the real and spiritual leadership of the Communist world. In 1966, by encouraging young people throughout China to 'Bombard the headquarters', Chairman Mao had unleashed a rabble of Red Guards who rampaged throughout China, smashing 'the four olds' (old habits, old culture, old customs and the old habits of the exploiting classes), breaking pianists' hands, burning books and paintings and personal photographs, forcing surgeons to clean hospital lavatories, teachers to wear dunce's hats, and terrifying many elderly intellectuals to the point of suicide. Referring to the great sixteenth-century novel *Journey to the West*, in which a mischievous monkey stirs up trouble wherever he goes, Mao said he wanted to create 'great disorder under heaven' in order to achieve 'great order under heaven'.[10]

In a message written in August 1966 to the Red Guards of the Middle School attached to Qinghua University in Beijing, whose youth is apparent from their address, he wrote thanking them for sending him their 'big character poster' in which they expressed their anger at and denunciation of 'all landlords, bourgeois, imperialists, revisionists, and their running dogs who exploit and oppress workers, peasants, revolutionary intellectuals and revolutionary parties and groupings'. He noted, 'You say it is right to rebel against reactionaries: I enthusiastically support you.'[11]

With Mao encouraging schoolchildren to rebel in 1966, many cities fell into a state of near anarchy. Faced with a dangerous breakdown in public order, the role of the People's Liberation Army, led by Mao's heir-apparent Lin Biao, was somewhat ambivalent. On the one hand it was needed to quell the worst excesses, as when fifty-seven different and fiercely ideologically opposed Red Guard factions in the city of Wuhan fought each other, and on the other, it was to take the lead in supporting the population in its smashing of

34. Putting up 'big character' posters criticizing Confucius and Lin Biao, 1976

the four olds, bombardment of the headquarters and carrying out the line struggle, class struggle and various other struggles.

As a gesture of loyalty, Lin Biao compiled the *Little Red Book* or *Quotations from Chairman Mao* as a useful source of slogans (and something to wave threateningly) in 1967, of which 350 million copies were printed. And though his power could have been strengthened by the realization in 1967 that the national economy could not survive the raging civil war and that the People's Liberation Army would have to take control in key factories and military installations, the continuing factional struggles at the highest level, often provoked and continued by Chairman Mao, threatened his position.

The official line in China is that, perhaps convinced he was being sidelined by the Chairman, Lin Biao took part with his son in several plots against Chairman Mao, to shoot him or attack his personal train with flame-throwers, rockets and anti-aircraft guns or by dynamiting a bridge as the train went over it. The plans seem never to have left the drawing board but Lin Biao's daughter unwisely revealed the plot to Zhou Enlai and, in panic, Lin Biao's son rushed to his parents' luxury villa at the seaside, interrupting a lobster dinner, and drove them to the airport to flee. The plane crashed in Mongolia, possibly because it had run out of fuel, and it is assumed that Lin Biao was fleeing to the Soviet Union, another act of treachery against Chairman Mao. That this flight was a surprise is clear: in September, as Lin fled, small children were still practising their parades in Tiananmen Square for the October 1st National Day celebrations, which were subsequently cancelled.

In 1973, searches of Lin Biao's Beijing residence apparently revealed that he had been a 'closet Confucian'. The searchers found 'calligraphy, books and index cards containing scribbled notes and quotes' all referring, in a positive manner, to Confucius and Confucianism.[12] That summer, a campaign to 'Criticize Lin Biao, Criticize Confucius' was launched. It was said that Lin Biao had picked up 'his scheming and craftiness' and his 'double-dealer work-style' from Confucius. 'No sunlight enters Lin Biao's bedroom, it's all gloomy. Everything about him was Confucian, from his ideas to the way he

35. *Confucius behaving erratically, from a cartoon satirizing*
Confucianism, 1976

lived.' His bedroom was also said to contain 'espionage equipment for use in a fascist coup d'état' as well as quotations from Confucius and Mencius on the wall and hand-copied quotations from Confucius on filial piety.[13]

Nowhere in the Confucian classics is there any mention of a gloomy bedroom. One of Confucius' disciples said he was very clean and 'bleached by the autumn sun', which makes him sound quite a fresh-air fiend.[14] We also know that he was fussy and simply could not sit down if his mat was not straight, whilst Lin Biao's den filled with espionage equipment and Confucian index cards sounds rather untidy.[15] The folk legend of Lin Biao in his dark bedroom persisted, for I can remember studying posters attacking Lin Biao in Tianjin Railway Station in the autumn of 1975 whilst waiting endlessly for the Public Security Bureau to check my voluminous papers and travel permit. They showed an ill-shaven man lying down on his bed, smoking, with his shoes on and a bubble above his head which

149

read: 'Thinks: Must Restore the Old Order', in other words, Confucianism. This was a particularly distasteful portrait, for removing your shoes and washing your feet before lying down in or on a bed is as essential to Chinese people as brushing their teeth last thing at night.

The outline of the plot to assassinate Chairman Mao, allegedly drawn up by Lin Biao's son, was distributed to senior Communist Party members in 1971. Apart from the flame-throwers and rockets, it was said also to contain rather incongruous attacks on Chairman Mao as a tyrant similar to the First Emperor. Slogans for the anti-Mao campaign were allegedly proposed: 'Down with the contemporary First Emperor' and 'Overthrow the feudal dynasty with the socialist shop-sign.' The parallels with the First Emperor continued, comparing his unification of China in 221 BC and Mao's victory of 1949 which had ended decades of civil war: 'Of course we do not deny his [Mao's] historical role in unifying China. Precisely because of this, in the history of our revolution, we have given him the trust and respect he deserves.' However, Mao was accused of betraying this trust: 'He is not a true Marxist-Leninist but the biggest feudal tyrant in Chinese history who, under the guise of Marxism-Leninism, follows the doctrines of Confucius and Mencius, and implements the laws of the First Emperor.'[16] It is hard to see how the doctrines of Confucius and the laws of the First Emperor could be combined, but since the publication of these (probably forged) accusations implied that Lin Biao and his fellow-plotters were obsessively opposed to the First Emperor, historians keen to please Chairman Mao were quick to see the need to 'reassess' the First Emperor.

As early as 1972, when the potential of this new interpretation of history began to emerge, the egregious Guo Moruo produced an essay on Chinese history in which he suggested, contrary to his previous view, that the First Emperor had been a positive historical figure. His argument was based on the Marxist-Leninist view of the stages of human history. The move from 'ancient society' to 'feudalism' was the beginning of the process (always expressed in economic terms) towards a capitalist society. The demise of the latter was confidently expected when contradictions within capitalism would become so acute that the alienated and oppressed workers would, through class struggle, eventually seize power and establish a new socialist society. According to Guo Moruo, the First Emperor had been instrumental in pushing history onwards, replacing a slave society with a feudal society, not in itself a 'good thing' but an essential movement towards capitalism and, eventually, the paradise of socialism. 'Swindlers' attacked the First Emperor's 'revolution', expressing a 'reactionary viewpoint which obstructed the advance of history'.[17]

Guo Moruo's article was first published in the major Chinese archaeological journal *Wenwu*, or *Cultural Relics*, but it must have found favour with the leadership for it was reprinted two months later, in July 1972, in *Red Flag*, the organ of the People's Liberation Army, which had a far wider readership and greater political prestige. No one seems to have pointed out that Guo's opinions were not strictly in accord with Marxist dialectical materialism, for to single out an emperor as a positive role model in the advance of history was in direct contradiction to the fundamental premise that the people, and the people alone, were the motive force in history.[18]

The campaign to 'Criticize Lin Biao, Criticize Confucius' was extended in 1974 and given the new title 'Criticize Confucianism, Appraise Legalism' after Mao had written in the winter of 1973 that 'All reactionary classes ... venerate Confucianism and oppose

Legalism, and oppose [the First Emperor].'[19] Just as Lin Biao and his family had allegedly plotted to attack Chairman Mao for behaving like the First Emperor, so a broad barrage of attacks on Lin Biao sought to show him as a direct descendant of the Confucian scholars who had opposed the First Emperor, as well as broadening the picture of the Confucian versus Legalist line struggle during the First Emperor's rule.

Publications supporting the 'Criticize Lin Biao, Criticize Confucius' campaign covered a range of issues. One essay, published in *Red Flag* in 1974, discussed an archaeological discovery of a number of bamboo-slip 'books' from two tombs '2,100 years'' old, dating from soon after the First Emperor's burning of the books. Fortunately for the archaeologists of the time, the books were mostly 'works about military affairs, and while there are some works by other pre-Qin philosophers, there are no Confucian classics at all'. Thus, according to the rhetoric of the time, 'with the concern of both the Party and the broad masses, the bamboo slips ... were immediately put in order scientifically and they are being further studied during the movement criticizing Lin Biao and Confucius'. In 1974, no writer could continue without praising Chairman Mao and the Cultural Revolution, so the paragraph concluded with a typical piece of political rhetoric: 'This is another new achievement made by our cultural relics workers and archaeologists since the Great Proletarian Cultural Revolution under the guidance of Chairman Mao's revolutionary line.'[20]

One of the bamboo-slip documents discovered was *The Art of War* by Sunzi, a text greatly admired by Chairman Mao, apparently studied by the Pentagon in an effort to understand guerrilla warfare and recently popular amongst management consultants.[21]

The significance of the find in terms of literary history was that this was an early copy, closer to the time of original compilation than any others, and it included passages since lost as well as variant wordings. The political significance of its discovery in 1974 was that the text could be adopted as a 'Legalist' text. Its survival also helpfully demonstrated the significance of the First Emperor's burning of the books as a well-directed and well-deserved attack on Confucianism, the ideology of the 'remnant forces of the slave-owning aristocrats'.

The Art of War was probably written in the fourth century BC, though it is variously attributed to Sun Bin (*c.* 350 BC) and Sun Wu (*c.* 500 BC). Well known in the West through the translation by Lionel Giles first published in 1910, it is full of pithy recommendations: 'All warfare is deception', 'Hold back to entice the enemy', 'Attack where he is unprepared, appear where you are not expected', 'If he is taking his ease, give him no rest. If his troops are united, separate them.' But it also takes a fairly high moral line on whether rulers are 'imbued with moral law' and thus worthy to be followed. The pro-Legalists of the Cultural Revolution, however, declared that Sunzi 'clearly pointed out the impracticability of "advocating humaneness and righteousness, performing rites and music, and wearing robes as a means to prevent disputes and fights" as trumpeted by the Confucians, and advocated "settlement by warfare"'. Though Sunzi actually served in another state and some time before the First Emperor, he is described as having 'vociferously affirmed the necessity of the act of unification' of the First Emperor.[22]

These newly excavated texts were used to demonstrate the fact that, far from burning books in order to 'destroy culture', the First Emperor 'evinced an attitude of protecting all progressive culture'. It was the Confucians and the 'reactionary rulers' who presided

36. Smashing the old, 1976

over textual loss, of military works and of 'books on medicine and forestry' that had been recorded in the catalogue of the Han imperial library but had not 'been passed down to the present'. Ending with quotations from Lenin in praise of Engels, the *Red Flag* article concluded that the First Emperor's 'book burning was a necessary measure during the process of the dictatorship of one exploiting class replacing another'.

Personal attacks on 'the renegade' Lin Biao in the campaign included an account of a trip he made. 'In May 1960 he went on a pilgrimage to pay homage to the so-called Temple of Meng's wife. This completely exposed Lin Biao's repulsive counter-revolutionary face.' Not far from the dramatic point where the Great Wall reaches the East China Sea at Shanhaiguan, stands a small temple devoted to the memory of the faithful wife whose husband had been conscripted by the First Emperor to work on the building of the Great Wall. When she reached the end of the Great Wall at the sea shore and learned that her husband had suffered great hardship and died, she wept until her tears caused the Wall to crumble. In visiting this well-known tourist destination, or making a 'pilgrimage', a particularly sinister activity from the extreme anti-religious viewpoint of the Cultural Revolution when a favourite activity of the Red Guards was to destroy all temples that had not been closed on Zhou Enlai's orders, Lin Biao was indirectly attacking the First Emperor yet again.[23]

An article published in the *People's Daily* on 25 December 1973 set out to destroy the legend of Meng's wife (and thereby attack Lin Biao for his pilgrimage to her temple), since the writer felt that 'when we appraise the First Emperor from the historical materialist viewpoint, we must make the truth clear by identifying false historical material'. The writer suggested that the legend grew up only in the Tang dynasty (AD 618–907) and that it was based upon a story recounted in texts dating back to five centuries before the First Emperor. The original story was that of a woman whose husband was killed in battle. When she heard the news, she wept and 'her wailing shook the city wall and caused a corner of it to crumble'. The writer continued, 'It is obviously preposterous to claim that a woman's wailing could cause a city wall to crumble. But as a folk tale, it reflects the spirit of resistance of the people against heavy compulsory labour service' – which of course it doesn't if it is based upon a husband's death in battle, rather than the later legend of Meng's wife.[24]

Finally, an essay published in *Red Flag* in December 1973 attempted to explain 'why Lin Biao reviled the First Emperor', a necessary logical exercise in the defence of Chairman Mao against the treason of his heir-apparent. The first paragraph reads as follows: 'Why did the bourgeois careerist, conspirator, counter-revolutionary hypocrite, renegade and traitor revile the First Emperor without restraint? Why did he maliciously attack "the burning of the books and the burying of the Confucian scholars alive" and other progressive measures adopted by the First Emperor? If we first use the class viewpoint and method of class analysis of Marxism to correctly analyse the First Emperor's reform spirit and the series of momentous measures he put into effect, and then look at the conditions under which Lin Biao attacked and reviled the First Emperor, we can get a clear picture of Lin Biao's sinister and counter-revolutionary political objective in reviling the First Emperor.'

Though the essay hardly seems worth reading beyond that first paragraph of round condemnation, it subsequently explains that Lin Biao's intention 'was for the purpose of opposing progress and opposing revolution' because, 'as an agent of the overthrown landlord and bourgeois classes', he hated the success of Chairman Mao's Great Proletarian Cultural Revolution. However, despite his counter-revolutionary howls for the liberation of landlords, like a 'mantis which tried to stop a cart with its arms', he was smashed to pieces by the forward-rolling wheel of revolutionary history.

Lin Biao was further accused of being opposed to revolutionary violence, an odd stance for the Head of the People's Liberation Army but one that is explained by the fact that he clung instead to counter-revolutionary violence. His ultimate aim was the restoration of capitalism as he 'drove in reverse gear, advocated restoration and bucked the tide of historical development' only to be 'smashed to bits under the mailed fists of the proletarian dictatorship'.[25] (This sort of garbled metaphor is very characteristic of the language of the Cultural Revolution, with its catch-phrases such as 'overthrowing the rightist revisionist wind on the cultural front'. I am nostalgically fond of the crazy rhetoric and look forward to a proper study of Chairman Mao's mixed metaphors.)

The language is garbled and so, too, is the message. A relatively simple power struggle and a possible failed coup d'état are not elucidated or explained by reference to the activities of the First Emperor over 2,000 years earlier. Some authorities consider that the whole 'Criticize Lin Biao, Criticize Confucius' campaign was not actually directed at Lin Biao, who was already dead, but against the urbane survivor, Zhou Enlai. Similarly, the next campaign, launched in 1975 against 'capitulationism' but expressed through criticism of the famous seventeenth-century historical novel, *The Water Margin*, was also said to be directed against Zhou Enlai.[26] These double-blind attacks are characteristic of an approach frequently used throughout Chinese history and described as 'pointing at the mulberry to revile the ash'.[27] From the time of the burning of the books and the burying of the scholars to that of the Qianlong emperor, direct criticism of the emperor or his administration was extremely dangerous, so scholars and critics resorted to indirect or veiled attacks. This was often coupled with the Confucian method of 'using the past to attack the present', both lines used in the positive reappraisal of the First Emperor in order to attack Lin Biao (and/or Zhou Enlai).

Earlier leaders who had been attacked for cruelty and therefore compared with the First Emperor included the first emperor of the Sui dynasty (AD 581–618). He, too, united the Chinese empire which, since the fall of the Han in AD 220, had been divided into numerous separate small states. Like the First Emperor, he had ordered massive reconstruction of the Great Wall and the Grand Canal, and the dynasty he founded did not survive beyond the second generation. Like the First Emperor, too, his short-lived reign, typically characterized as brutal, paved the way for one of China's greatest dynasties, that of the Tang which lasted from AD 618 to 907.[28] Another 'villain' in traditional Chinese historiography was Zhu Yuanzhang, who founded the Ming dynasty (1368–1644) having risen from a background of unrelenting and murderous poverty to fight with rebel armies determined to overthrow the alien Mongol dynasty. His reign was different, for the early Ming was a period of considerable enlightenment with free schools for poor boys and a careful campaign of liberal taxation to get land that had been abandoned during the fighting back into cultivation. And the Ming dynasty proved quite long-lasting. It was only his increasing personal paranoia and subsequent cruelty that earned him his posthumous reputation. The poverty of his childhood – his father, mother and elder brother died during a famine in 1344 – led some to compare him with Chairman Mao, whose peasant background was well known, although his family was by no means as poor as that of Zhu Yuanzhang.[29]

A fine biography of the first Ming emperor by the historian Wu Han was published in Shanghai in 1949. Later editions, published after Chairman Mao had led the Communist Party to power, were revised in the light of changing political views of history when Chairman Mao himself, in self-conscious identification with the Ming emperor, suggested that he depict him in a more favourable light.[30] Wu Han became deputy mayor of Beijing and, increasingly concerned by Chairman Mao's refusal to tolerate criticism or admit errors, adopted the age-old method of 'using the past to criticize the present' and 'pointing at the mulberry tree to revile the ash'. In

1960, at a time of grave food shortages caused partly by the falsification of grain figures by unscrupulous local officials, he wrote a Peking opera about an upright Ming official who dared to criticize the Ming emperor and pleaded on behalf of suffering peasants. In 1965, articles criticizing the historian began to appear in the *People's Daily* and other newspapers, in what is commonly regarded as the opening campaign of Chairman Mao's Great Proletarian Cultural Revolution (1966–76), fought at this stage, like the campaign for the First Emperor and against Lin Biao, on the basis of arguments about Chinese history.[31]

The campaign to 'Criticize Lin Biao, Criticize Confucius', with its constant references to the First Emperor, had begun to lose momentum when, in 1974, the remarkable discovery of the Buried Army was made. Immediately the First Emperor assumed another status. No longer fought over as inhumane and brutal or progressive and empowering, he became an archaeological hero, his tomb 'another wonder of the world and a treasure house of [the] ancient spiritual civilization of mankind', as an early publication described it.[32] Attention shifted from Lin Biao and Confucius to the tomb and its inhabitant, and there it has remained ever since.

Notes

Introduction

1. Li Xueqin, *Eastern Zhou and Qin Civilizations*, trans. K. C. Chang (New Haven, Yale University Press, 1985), p. 222. Though situated on the edge of 'China', it has been argued that the local population would have been thoroughly sinified by contact and intermarriage: see Nicola di Cosmo, 'The Northern Frontier in Pre-Imperial China', in Michael Loewe and Edward L. Shaughnessy (eds.), *The Cambridge History of Ancient China: From the Origins of Civilization to 221 BC* (Cambridge, Cambridge University Press, 1999), pp. 885–966.

2. George Babcock Cressey, *China's Geographic Foundations: A Survey of the Land and Its People* (New York, McGraw-Hill, 1934), pp. 184–8.

3. For maps of the Qin and Han domains see Valerie Hansen, *The Open Empire: A History of China to 1600* (New York, Norton, 2000), pp. 98 and 113.

4. Jessica Rawson, *Ancient China: Art and Archaeology* (London, British Museum, 1980), p. 40. For a more detailed account of the Neolithic and the increasing number of new sites discovered, see Chang Kwang-chih, 'China on the Eve of

the Historical Period', in Loewe and Shaughnessy 1999, pp. 48–65.

5. Chang in Loewe and Shaughnessy 1999, p. 72.

6. David Keightley, 'The Shang: China's First Historical Dynasty', in Loewe and Shaughnessy 1999, p. 248.

7. The compilers of *The Historical Atlas of China*, Vol. 1 (Shanghai, Ditu chubanshe, 1982), base their map on traditional historiographical sources, oracle-bone references and archaeological sites but indicate no boundaries: see pp. 9–10.

8. Edward L. Shaughnessy, 'Western Zhou History', in Loewe and Shaughnessy 1999, pp. 302–7.

9. *Historical Atlas of China*, Vol. 1, 1982, pp. 15–16.

10. Edward L. Shaughnessy in Loewe and Shaughnessy 1999, pp. 318 *et seq.*

11. Hsu Cho-yun, 'The Spring and Autumn Period', in Loewe and Shaughnessy 1999, p. 545.

12. Mark Edward Lewis, 'Warring States Political History', in Loewe and Shaughnessy 1999, p. 587.

13. Hansen 2000, pp. 36–8.

14. Corinne Debaine-Francfort, *The Search for Ancient China* (London, Thames and Hudson, 1999), pp. 79–83.

15. Mark Elvin, *The Retreat of the Elephants: An Environmental History of China* (New Haven, Yale University Press, 2004), p. 24. Captured elephants were taught to dance, see Peng Jie, 'A brief history of dancing elephants', *Xi yu wenwu*, vol 1, p. 49–54.

16. Elvin 2004, pp. 42 and 25.

17. Elvin 2004, pp. 121–2.

18. Derk Bodde, 'The State and Empire of Ch'in', in Denis Twitchett and Michael Loewe (eds.), *The Cambridge History of China*, Vol. 1, *The Ch'in and Han Empires, 221 BC–AD 220* (Cambridge, Cambridge University Press, 1986), p. 46.

19. Elvin 2004, p. 122.

20. Bodde in Twitchett and Loewe 1986, p. 65.

21. Francesca Bray, 'Agriculture', in Joseph Needham (ed.), *Science and Civilization in China*, Vol. 6, *Biology and Biological Technology* Part 2, *Agriculture* (Cambridge, Cambridge University Press, 1984), pp. 141–3, 147, 217, 222 and 329.

22. Bray in Needham 1984, p. 288.

23. Bray in Needham 1984, pp. 292–3.

24. Elvin 2004, pp. 105–7.

25. Shen Congwen, *Zhongguo gudai fushi yanjiu/Research into Ancient Chinese Dress and Ornament* (Hong Kong, Shangwu yinshuguan, 1981), fig. 20.

26. Shen 1981, figs. 22–3, 26 and 31.

27. K. C. Chang (ed.), *Food in Chinese Culture* (New Haven, Yale University Press, 1977), p. 80.

28. This may have been partly due to greater forest and shrub cover at the time.

29. K. C. Chang 1977, p. 28.

30. K. C. Chang 1977, pp. 27–8.

31. K. C. Chang 1977, pp. 29–30.

32. K. C. Chang 1977, p. 31.

33. David Hawkes, *The Songs of the South: An Ancient Chinese Anthology* (Harmondsworth, Penguin, 1985), pp. 107 and 111.

34. K. C. Chang 1977, p. 37.

35. Bray 1984, p. 415, and J. J. L. Duyvendak, *The Book of Lord Shang: A Classic of the Chinese School of Law* (London, Probsthain, 1963), p. 48.

Chapter 1

1. Denis Twitchett and Michael Loewe (eds.), *The Cambridge History of China*, Vol. 1, *The Ch'in and Han Empires, 221 BC–AD 220* (Cambridge, Cambridge University Press, 1986), p. 40.

2. Li Xueqin, *Eastern Zhou and Qin Civilizations*, trans. K. C. Chang (New Haven, Yale University Press, 1984), p. 222. For an alternative analysis, see Nicola di Cosmo, 'The Northern Frontier in Pre-Imperial China', in Michael Loewe and Edward Shaughnessy (eds.), *The Cambridge History of Ancient China: From the Origins of Civilization to 221 BC* (Cambridge, Cambridge University Press, 1999), pp. 885–966.

3. There is a recent biography of the First Emperor based on major Chinese sources, Jonathan Clements, *The First Emperor of China* (Stroud, Sutton Publishing, 2006).

4. Hans Bielenstein, 'Wang Mang, the Restoration of the Han Dynasty, and Later Han', in Twitchett and Loewe 1986, p. 259.

5. Lü Buwei (in Wade-Giles romanization, Lü Pu-wei)'s titles have been varying translated in different texts. He also held different posts at different times although, until his disgrace, they were all very important. To avoid confusion I have chosen the title Prime Minister for him. See Michael Loewe, *A Biographical Dictionary of the Qin, Former Han and Xin*

Periods (221 BC–AD 24) (Leiden, Brill, 2000), pp. 420–1, and William H. Nienhauser Jnr (ed.), *The Grand Scribe's Records*, Vol. 1, *Basic Annals of Pre-Han China* (Bloomington, Indiana University Press, 1994), p. 127, where he is referred to as Chancellor.

6. David Shepherd Nivison, 'The Classical Philosophical Writings', in Twitchett and Loewe 1986, p. 808, and Cho-yun Hsu, 'The Spring and Autumn Period', in Twitchett and Loewe 1986, p. 582.

7. From the *Zhanguo ce/Records of the Warring States*, J. I. Crump, *Chan-kuo tse* (Oxford, Clarendon Press), 1970, p. 137.

8. Derk Bodde, 'The State and Empire of Ch'in', in Twitchett and Loewe 1986, pp. 42–3.

9. Derk Bodde, *Statesman, Patriot and General in Ancient China: Three Shi Ji Biographies of the Qin Dynasty* (New Haven, American Oriental Society, 1940), p. 7.

10. Loewe 2000, p. 421: see also Jeffrey Riegel and John Knoblock, *The Annals of Lü Buwei, Lu shi chunqiu: complete translation and study* (Stanford, Stanford University Press), 2000.

11. The quotations taken from Yang Hsien-I and Gladys Yang, *Records of the Historian* (Hong Kong, Commercial Press, 1974), reprinted in Li Yu-ning, *The First Emperor of China: The Politics of Historiography* (White Plains, International Arts and Sciences Press, 1975) (*Chinese Studies in History*, Vol. VIII, Nos. 1–2), p. 264.

12. Derk Bodde, *China's First Unifier: A Study of the Ch'in Dynasty as Seen in the Life of Li Ssu* (Hong Kong, Hong Kong University Press, 1967), p. 119.

13. Bodde 1967, pp. 4–5.

14. Yang Hsien-I and Gladys Yang in Li 1975, pp. 267–8.
15. Yang Hsien-I and Gladys Yang in Li 1975, pp. 268–70.
16. Derk Bodde, 'The State and Empire of Ch'in', in Twitchett and Loewe, 1986, pp. 53–4. I understand that the current favoured translation in academic circles is 'Divine Thearch.'
17. Bodde in Twitchett and Loewe 1986, pp. 20–1.
18. From 1045 when it overthrew the Shang dynasty, until about the 4th century BC, the Zhou dynasty effectively ruled China. From the 4th century BC, as other states rose to challenge, the Zhou ruling house staggered on until 256 BC when it was defeated by the state of Qin.
19. Yang Hsien-I and Gladys Yang in Li 1975, p. 269. The Manchus who founded the Qing dynasty (1644–1911) took earth as their element with its associated colour of yellow.
20. Quoted in Nienhauser 1994, p. 136, note 132.
21. Yang Hsien-I and Gladys Yang in Li 1975, p. 269.
22. Standardization of all these items and the coinage will be discussed in Chapter 8.
23. Yang Hsien-I and Gladys Yang in Li 1975, p. 270.
24. Bodde in Twitchett and Loewe 1986, p. 65.
25. Jessica Rawson and Evelyn Rawski (eds.), *China: The Three Emperors* (London, Royal Academy, 2006), contains many illustrations of the paintings of imperial trips. Not all emperors were as keen to ascend endless sacred mountains: the Ming (1368–1644) were notoriously stay-at-home emperors.
26. Bodde in Twitchett and Loewe 1986, p. 68.
27. Yang Hsien-I and Gladys Yang in Li 1975, p. 271.
28. Yang Hsien-I and Gladys Yang in Li 1975, pp. 272–3.
29. Bodde 1967, p. 26.

Chapter 2

1. The text by Sima Qian (Wade-Giles Ssu-ma Ch'ien) has been translated into English under various titles: *Records of the Grand Historian of China* in Burton Watson's version (1961); *Records of the Historian* in Yang Hsien-I and Gladys Yang's version (1974), and, in the most recent translation edited by William H. Nienhauser Jnr (1994), *The Grand Scribe's Records*.

2. Valerie Hansen, *The Open Empire: A History of China to 1600* (New York, Norton, 2000), pp. 110–11.

3. For early book formats see Tsien Tsuen-hsuin, *Written on Bamboo and Silk: The Beginnings of Chinese Books and Inscriptions* (Chicago, University of Chicago Press, 2004).

4. Hansen 2000, p. 111.

5. The importance of the *Han shu* or *History of the Former Han* in the creation of traditional Chinese historical writing is also significant: see Denis Twitchett and Michael Loewe (eds.), *The Cambridge History of China*, Vol. 1, *The Ch'in and Han Empires, 221 BC–AD 220* (Cambridge, Cambridge University Press, 1986), p. 4.

6. Hans Bielenstein, 'Wang Mang, the Restoration of the Han Dynasty, and Later Han', in Twitchett and Loewe 1986, p. 259.

7. Nienhauser 1994, p. vii.

8. Hansen 2000, p. 110.

9. Nienhauser 1994, p. ix, though I'm assuming that 'stone chambers and bronze bookcases' might refer to materials rather than furniture.

10. Nienhauser 1994, pp. xiii–xiv.

11. Li Yu-ning (ed.), *The First Emperor of China: The Politics of Historiography*, *Chinese Studies in History*, Vol. VIII, Nos. 1–2 (White Plains, International Arts and Sciences Press, 1975), p. 316.

12. William Theodore de Bary in Li 1975, pp. 317–18.

13. Michael Loewe, *A Biographical Dictionary of the Qin, Former Han and Xin Periods, 221 BC–AD 24* (Leiden, Brill, 2000), p. 654.

Chapter 3

1. The Councillor's name was Li Si (or Li Ssu in the Wade-Giles romanization system). He held many official positions in his life: 'Senior Scribe', 'Alien Minister', 'Minister of Justice' and 'Grand Councillor' in Bodde's translation, and 'Superintendent of Trials' and 'Chancellor' in Loewe's version. For the sake of simplicity, I have chosen to call him Councillor throughout. Derk Bodde, *China's First Unifier: A Study of the Ch'in Dynasty as Seen in the Life of Li Ssu, ?280–208 BC* (Hong Kong, Hong Kong University Press, 1967), pp. 21–2; and Michael Loewe, *A Biographical Dictionary of the Qin, Former Han and Xin Periods, 221 BC–AD 24* (Leiden, Brill, 2000), p. 228.

2. Bodde 1967, p. 13.

3. Bodde 1967, pp. 18–21.

4. The question of the reliability of *The Grand Scribe's Records* is described in the Chapter 2.

5. Bodde 1967, p. 26.

6. Yang Hsien-I and Gladys Yang in Li Yu-ning, *The First Emperor of China: The Politics of Historiography, Chinese Studies in History*, Vol. VIII, Nos. 1–2 (White Plains, International Arts and Sciences Press, 1975), p. 266.

7. Victor Mair, *Chinese Lives*, forthcoming.

8. William H. Nienhauser Jnr (ed.), *The Grand Scribe's Records*, Vol. 7, *The Memoirs of Pre-Han China* (Bloomington, Indiana University Press, 1994), p. 366.

9. Bodde 1967, p. 49.

Chapter 4

1. London, Allen and Unwin, 1946. James Legge had already published many ancient Chinese texts in his seven-volume series, *The Chinese Classics* (Oxford, 1893), but these were used only as scholarly references; Waley's great contribution was to produce accessible translations from the Chinese which sold very widely at the time.

2. David Shepherd Nivison, 'The Classical Philosophical Writings', in Michael Loewe and Edward L. Shaughnessy (eds.), *The Cambridge History of Ancient China: From the Origins of Civilization to 221 BC* (Cambridge, Cambridge University Press, 1999), p. 745. This is a brilliant essay to which I am much indebted.

3. Confucius, *The Analects*, trans. and with annotations by D. C. Lau (Harmondsworth, Penguin, 1979), pp. 21–2. For an explanation on the variants on the titles see note 4 chapter 7.

4. Nivison in Loewe and Shaughnessy 1999, p. 746.

5. Edwin O. Reischauer and John K. Fairbank, *East Asia: The Great Tradition* (Boston, Houghton Mifflin, 1960), p. 65.

6. Nivison in Loewe and Shaughnessy 1999, p. 746.

7. James Legge, *The Four Books* (Shanghai, The China Book Company, n.d.), Book XVII, p. 253. The rather aggressive gift, intended to provoke the desired reaction, is reminiscent of pig-giving ceremonies (*moka*) in Papua New Guinea. Confucius' ploy reminds me of *Cranford*.

8. Lau 1979, pp. 102–3.

9. The first part of this chapter owes much to Nivison in Loewe and Shaughnessy 1999, pp. 749–55; see also Lau 1979, p. 135.

10. Lau 1979, p. 114.

11. Lau 1979, pp. 118–19; the last phrase seems to me a bit of a non-sequitur.

12. Nivison in Loewe and Shaughnessy 1999, pp. 782–3.

13. Nivison in Loewe and Shaughnessy 1999, p. 775.

14. Nivison in Loewe and Shaughnessy 1999, p. 774.

15. Valerie Hansen, *The Open Empire: A History of China to 1600* (New York, Norton, 2000), p. 89.

16. Hansen 2000, p. 83. Taoism derives from the old Wade-Giles romanization, Daoism from the newer pinyin romanization. I shall use Daoism, since it fits better with today's romanization of the names of the texts and also indicates more accurately how it should be pronounced.

17. Hansen 2000, p. 84.

18. Hansen 2000, pp. 84–5, quoting from Victor Mair's translation of the *Daodejing* (New York, Bantam, 1990).

19. Hansen 2000, p. 90.

20. J. J. L. Duyvendak, *The Book of Lord Shang: A Classic of the Chinese School of Law* (London, Probsthain, 1963), p. 256. Duyvendak's mistake over numbers may have been missed in 1928 but it did not escape the eagle eye of the Profile proofreader, Carol Anderson.

21. Duyvendak 1963, p. 57.

22. It is interesting to reflect on how this system of mutual responsibility persisted throughout Chinese history. Even today, the family of an executed criminal is charged for the bullet that ends his life, and the Cultural Revolution (1966–76) was characterized by much denunciation of neighbours and family members.

23. Duyvendak 1963, pp. 250–1.

24. Duyvendak 1963, p. 257.

25. Hansen 2000, p. 102.

26. Michael Loewe, 'The Heritage Left to the Empires', in Loewe and Shaughnessy 1999, pp. 1003–4.

Chapter 5

1. A. F. P. Hulsewe, *Remnants of Ch'in Law* (Leiden, Brill, 1985), p. 1. This translation of the excavated legal texts of the Qin is fascinating in its detail and I have relied greatly upon it.

2. Li Xueqin, *Eastern Zhou and Qin Civilizations*, trans. K. C. Chang (New Haven, Yale University Press, 1985), pp. 425–30.

3. Hulsewe 1985, p. 21.

4. Hulsewe 1985, p. 32.

5. Hulsewe 1985, pp. 26–8.

6. Hulsewe 1985, pp. 162–3.
7. Hulsewe 1985, pp. 59–61.
8. During the Cultural Revolution, everyone was issued with grain coupons for a monthly ration. They also received cloth coupons, oil coupons and egg coupons as all these commodities were rationed. As a foreign student, I received cloth coupons but we were not given grain coupons as we didn't eat enough rice to make a dent in the national stockpile.
9. Hulsewe 1985, p. 55. The question of weights and measures in China's history is immensely complex.
10. I do not know whether that is still the case, but I recently noticed a similar height mark by the ticket office in the Beijing railway station.
11. Hulsewe 1985, p. 122.
12. Hulsewe 1985, p. 166.
13. Hulsewe 1985, p. 198.
14. Hulsewe 1985, p. 200.
15. Only a couple of decades ago, a senior official in the Nanjing Museum who felt wronged by the Museum administration hanged himself in the Museum. His family refused to allow the body to be moved for some time, in support of his protest.
16. Hulsewe 1985, pp. 14–17.
17. Hulsewe 1985, p. 18.

Chapter 6

1. P. du Halde, *The General History of China*, trans. R. Brookes (London, 1736), Vol. 1, p. 29.

2. Du Halde 1736, Vol. 2, pp. 76–7.

3. James Boswell, *Boswell's Life of Johnson* (London, Oxford University Press, 1953), p. 929.

4. George Staunton, *An Authentic Account of an Embassy from the King of Great Britain to the Emperor of China* [1797] (Dublin, 1798), Vol. 2, pp. 73–4.

5. Jorge Luis Borges, 'The Wall and the Books', trans. James E. Irby, in Daniel Schwarz, *The Great Wall of China* (London, Thames and Hudson, 1990), p. 10.

6. C. P. Fitzgerald, *China: A Short Cultural History* (London, Cresset Press, 1935), p. 519.

7. Julia Lovell, *The Great Wall: China against the World, 1000 BC–AD 2000* (London, Atlantic Books, 2006), p. 41.

8. A li or Chinese mile is about one-third of an English mile. The use of the term 'ten thousand' is commonly used in China to refer to something large or long and should not be taken as an accurate measurement. The Great Wall was referred to as the 'ten-thousand li wall' from this period.

9. Shi Ji 88, quoted in Nicola di Cosmo, *Ancient China and Its Enemies: The Rise of Nomadic Power in East Asian History* (Cambridge, Cambridge University Press, 2002), p. 175.

10. Views expressed by Owen Lattimore as described in Joseph Needham, *Science and Civilization in China*, Vol. 1, *Introductory Orientations* (Cambridge, Cambridge University Press, 1954), p. 100. For 'cap and girdle', see Arthur Waldron, *The Great Wall of China: From History to Myth* (Cambridge, Cambridge University Press, 1990), p. 23.

11. Di Cosmo 2002, p. 102.

12. Waldron 1990, p. 17.

13. Waldron 1990, p. 28.
14. A. P. Hulsewe, 'Ch'in and Han Law', in Denis Twitchett and Michael Loewe (eds.), *The Cambridge History of China*, Vol. 1, *The Ch'in and Han Empires 221 BC–AD 220* (Cambridge, Cambridge University Press, 1986), p. 537. Hulsewe explains that the age limits varied from 15 to 23 and 56 to 60 at various times.
15. Hulsewe in Twitchett and Loewe 1986, p. 538.
16. Waldron 1990, pp. 197–201.
17. William H. Nienhauser Jnr (ed.), *The Grand Scribe's Records*, Vol. 7, *The Memoirs of Pre-Han China* (Bloomington, Indiana University Press, 1994), p. 366.

Chapter 7

1. Craig Clunas, *Superfluous Things: Material Culture and Social Status in Early Modern China* (Cambridge, Polity Press, 1991), p. 125.
2. Paul Demieville, 'Philosophy and Religion from Han to Sui', in Denis Twitchett and Michael Loewe (eds.), *The Cambridge History of China*, Vol. 1, *The Ch'in and Han Empires, 221 BC–AD 220* (Cambridge, Cambridge University Press, 1986), p. 813.
3. Yang Hsien-I and Gladys Yang, *Records of the Historian* (Hong Kong, Commercial Press, 1974), reprinted in Li Yu-ning (ed.), *The First Emperor of China: The Politics of Historiography* (White Plains, International Arts and Sciences Press, 1975), pp. 278–80.

4. The *Book of Songs*, *Shi Jing*, is also referred to as the *Classic of Songs*, *Book of Odes* or *Book of Poetry*. There have been many translations, most notably by Arthur Waley, *The Book of Songs* (London, 1937). The *Book of History*, *Shu Jing*, also known as the *Classic of Documents*, existed in two different versions in the second century BC and is thought to be largely composed of forgeries. Edwin O. Reischauer and John King Fairbank, *East Asia: The Great Tradition* (Boston, Houghton Mifflin, 1960), p. 65.

5. Jens Ostergard Peterson, 'Which Books Did the First Emperor of China Burn? On the Meaning of Pai Chia in Early Chinese Sources', *Monumenta Serica*, Vol. 63, 1995, p. 26.

6. Peterson 1995, pp. 2 *et seq.*

7. Nienhauser 1986, p. 144.

8. Li Xueqin, *Eastern Zhou and Qin Civilizations*, trans. K. C. Chang (New Haven, Yale University Press, 1985), p. 430.

9. Derk Bodde, 'The State and Empire of Ch'in', in Twitchett and Loewe 1986, p. 84.

10. Bodde in Twitchett and Loewe 1986, p. 71.

11. *Dijian tushuo*: see Julia K. Murray, 'Didactic Illustrations in Printed Books', in Cynthia J. Brokaw and Kai-wing Chow (eds.), *Printing and Book Culture in Late Imperial China* (Berkeley, University of California Press, 2005), pp. 419–27.

12. Yang Hsien-I and Gladys Yang in Li 1975, p. 282.

13. Nienhauser 1986, p. 150, note 159.

14. Ulrich Neininger, 'Burying the Scholars Alive: On the Origin of a Confucian Martyr's Legend', in Wolfram Eberhard *et al.*, *East Asian Civilizations 2* (Munich, Simon and Magiera, 1983), p. 133.

15. L. C. Goodrich, *The Literary Inquisition of Ch'ien-lung* [1935] (New York, Paragon Book Reprint Corporation, 1966), pp. 30–1.

16. Frances Wood, *Chinese Illustration* (London, British Library, 1985), pp. 40–1, and an entry for Ch'en Meng-lei in Arthur Hummel (ed.), *Eminent Chinese of the Ch'ing Period (1644–1912)* (Washington, US Government Printing Office, 1943–4), pp. 93–5.

17. Goodrich 1966, p. 207. Dismemberment of a corpse was a particularly cruel punishment both as a Confucian insult to one's parents who had provided the complete body and also because it was believed that the souls of the dismembered dead would wander unhappily for ever, trying to gather all the bits. For that reason, hanging was considered a less severe penalty than beheading.

18. Goodrich 1966, pp. 44–53.

19. Goodrich 1966, pp. 80–1.

20. Goodrich 1966, p. 42.

Chapter 8

1. Ulrich Neininger, 'Burying the Scholars: On the Origin of a Confucian Martyrs' Legend', in Wolfram Eberhard, Krzystof Gawlikowski and Carl Albrecht Seyschab (eds.), *East Asian Civilizations: New Attempts at Understanding Traditions, 2: Nation and Mythology* (n.p., Simon and Magiera, 1983), p. 126.

2. I am greatly indebted to Helen Wang for her expertise and have made much use of her essay on coins for the catalogue of

the forthcoming British Museum exhibition in the autumn of 2007.

3. A. F. P. Hulsewe, *Remnants of Ch'in Law* (Leiden, Brill, 1985), pp. 93–6. For more detail on weights and measures see A. F. P. Hulsewe, 'Weights and Measures in Ch'in Law', in Dieter Eikemeier and Herbert Franke (eds.), *State and Law in East Asia, Festschrift Karl Bunger* (Wiesbaden, Otto Harrasowitz, 1981), pp. 25–39. See also Li Xueqin, *Eastern Zhou and Qin Civilizations*, trans. K. C. Chang (New Haven, Yale University Press, 1985), p. 240.

4. Li Xueqin 1985, pp. 241–2, and Hulsewe 1985, p. 19. There are several reference books on the subject: see Endymion Wilkinson, *Chinese History: A Manual* (Cambridge, Harvard University Press, 1998), pp. 237–8, where he notes that a foot grew by 40 per cent between the Qin and the Qing, and that one planned supplement to a standard work never appeared, for reasons I can well understand.

5. Li Xueqin 1985, p. 245, and Hulsewe 1985, p. 19.

6. Joseph Needham, *Science and Civilization in China*, Vol. 4, *Physics and Physical Technology* Part 3, *Civil Engineering and Nautics* (Cambridge, Cambridge University Press, 1954–), pp. 5–6.

7. Needham 1954, Vol. 4, Part 3, p. 7, note.

8. Needham 1954, Vol. 4, Part 3, p. 15.

9. Needham 1954, Vol. 4, Part 3, pp. 8–10.

10. The difficulties of deciding quite what a foot was at different times in Chinese history have already been discussed: see Note 4. See Needham 1954, Vol. 4, Part 3, pp. 5–6 note.

11. I am simplifying this discussion to a point where scholars may be critical, but it is a pretty complex problem. For those interested in following scholarly research on the subject, consult William G. Boltz, 'Language and Writing', in Michael Loewe and Edward L. Shaughnessy (eds.), *The Cambridge History of Ancient China: From the Origins of Civilization to 221 BC* (Cambridge, Cambridge University Press, 1999), pp. 74–123, and Noel Barnard, 'The Nature of the Ch'in "Reform of the Scripts" as Reflected in Archaeological Documents Excavated under Conditions of Control', in David T. Roy and Tsuen-hsuin Tsien (eds.), *Ancient China: Studies in Early Civilization* (Hong Kong, Chinese University Press, 1978), pp. 181–213.

12. Barnard in Roy and Tsien 1978, p. 181.

Chapter 9

1. Herbert A. Giles, *A Chinese Biographical Dictionary* [1898] (Taipei, Literature House, 1962), p. 161.

2. Edward H. Schafer, 'Hunting Parks in China', *Journal of the Economic and Social History of the Orient*, Vol. 11, Part 1, 1968, pp. 321–2.

3. Schafer 1968, p. 322.

4. Schafer 1968, p. 323.

5. Schafer 1968, p. 324.

6. On the *Shuowen jiezi* dictionary, see Endymion Wilkinson, *Chinese History: A Manual* (Cambridge, Mass., Harvard University Press, 1998), p. 65.

7. Schafer 1968, pp. 331–2.

8. Joseph Needham, *Science and Civilization in China*, Vol. 6, *Biology and Biological Technology*, Part 1, *Botany* (Cambridge, Cambridge University Press, 1954–), pp. 418 and 463–5.

9. Needham Vol. 6, Part 1, p. 465.

10. Needham Vol. 6, Part 1, pp. 465–6.

11. Burton Watson, *Chinese Rhyme Prose: Poems in the Fu Form from the Han and Six Dynasties Periods* (New York, Columbia University Press, 1971), p. 37. I quote from his translation of Sima Xiangru's *fu*, 'The Shanglin [Supreme Forest] Park'.

12. Watson 1971, pp. 37–8.

13. Watson 1971, pp. 40–1.

14. Watson 1971, pp. 39–40.

15. Watson 1971, pp. 45–6.

16. Watson 1971, p. 45.

17. Yang Hsien-I and Gladys Yang, 'Basic Annals of Ch'in Shih-huang', in Li Yu-ning, *The First Emperor of China: The Politics of Historiography* (White Plains, International Arts and Sciences Press, 1975), p. 270.

18. Fu Xinian, Guo Daiheng, Liu Xujie *et al.*, *Chinese Architecture*, English text by Nancy S. Steinhardt (New Haven and Beijing, Yale University Press and New World Press, 2002), p. 41. Such 'travelling palaces' were also constructed in large numbers by the eighteenth-century Qing emperors: see Frances Wood, 'Imperial Architecture of the Qing: Palaces and Retreats', in Jessica Rawson and Evelyn Rawski (eds.), *China: The Three Emperors* (London, Royal Academy of Arts, 2005), p. 60.

19. Ying-shih Yu, 'Life and Immortality in the Mind of Han China', *Harvard Journal of Asiatic Studies*, Vol. 25, 1964–5, p. 91.

20. Without wishing to suggest that Chinese architecture was invariably 'multi-purpose', the same principles applied to buildings from grand to small throughout much of China's history. The main halls were oriented to face south, with enclosures forming courtyards and balanced on either side of the main axis. During the eighteenth century, the Beijing palace formerly occupied by the future Qianlong emperor was made into a temple, the Lamaist Yonglegong, for it was considered improper for a former imperial residence to be occupied by anyone else.

21. Fu Xinian *et al.* 2002, pp. 39–41.

22. William H. Nienhauser Jnr, *The Grand Scribe's Records*, Vol. 1 (Bloomington, Indiana University Press, 1994), p. 148, note 250.

23. Yang Hsien-I and Gladys Yang in Li Yu-ning 1975, p. 280.

24. Fu Xinian *et al.* 2002, p. 40. For the stepped effect, see Wang Tao, 'The Blueprint for the Zhongshan King's Graveyard', *East Asia Journal*, Vol. 1, No. 1, 2003, pp. 19–20.

25. Derk Bodde, 'The State and Empire of Ch'in', in Denis Twitchett and Michael Loewe (eds.), *The Cambridge History of China*, Vol. 1, *The Ch'in and Han Dynasties* (Cambridge, Cambridge University Press, 1986), p. 102.

26. Yang Hsien-I and Gladys Yang in Li Yu-ning 1975, p. 270.

27. Fu Xinian *et al.* 2002, p. 40.

Chapter 10

1. Michael Loewe, 'The Religious and Intellectual Background', in Denis Twitchett and Michael Loewe (eds.), *The Cambridge History of China*, Vol. 1, *The Ch'in and Han Empires 221 BC–AD 220* (Cambridge, Cambridge University Press, 1986), p. 715.

2. Donald Harper, 'Warring States Natural Philosophy and Occult Thought', in Michael Loewe and Edward Shaughnessy (eds.), *The Cambridge History of Ancient China: From the Origins of Civilization to 221 BC* (Cambridge, Cambridge University Press, 1999), p. 827.

3. Yang Hsien-I and Gladys Yang, 'Basic Annals', in Li Yu-ning, *The First Emperor of China: The Politics of Historiography* (White Plains, International Arts and Sciences Press, 1975), p. 274.

4. Yang Hsien-I and Gladys Yang in Li Yu-ning 1975, p. 282.

5. Yang Hsien-I and Gladys Yang in Li Yu-ning 1975, p. 283.

6. See Loewe in Twitchett and Loewe 1986, pp. 717–18.

7. A jade 'funeral suit' made for a princess who died in the late second century BC was exhibited in London in 1973–4: William Watson, *The Chinese Exhibition* (London, Royal Academy of Arts, 1973), pp. 100–1.

8. Ying-shih Yu, 'Life and Immortality in Han China', *Harvard Journal of Asiatic Studies*, Vol. 25, 1964–5, pp. 87–8.

9. Yu 1964–5, p. 91.

10. E. T. C. Werner, *A Dictionary of Chinese Mythology* (New York, Julian Press, 1961), pp. 341–52.

11. Yu 1964–5, p. 94.

12. Jacques Roi and Ou Yun Juei, 'Taoisme et les plantes d'immortalité', *Bulletin de l'Université de l'Aurore*, 1934, Second Series, Vol. 2, No. 4, p. 538.

13. Joseph Needham, *Science and Civilization in China*, Vol. 5, *Chemistry and Chemical Technology*, Part 2, *Spagyrical Discovery and Invention: Magisteries of Gold and Immortality* (Cambridge, Cambridge University Press, 1974), p. 122.

14. Roi and Ou 1934, pp. 540–3.

15. Jean Lévi, *Le Grand Empereur et ses automates* (Paris, Albin Michel, 1985), pp. 292–4. The *Oxford English Dictionary* has realgar as 'disulphide of arsenic', apparently related to red orpiment and 'the King's Yellow'.

16. Levi 1985, p. 295.

17. Derk Bodde, 'The State and Empire of Ch'in', in Twitchett and Loewe 1986, p. 27. No one has apparently weighed bamboo documents to find out just how many there would be in 30 kilos. I find this unusual method of measuring very endearing as it reminds me of my Chinese teacher at Cambridge who always calculated his library in feet and inches rather than by the number of volumes it contained.

Chapter 11

1. James Legge, *The Four Books* (Shanghai, China Book Company, n.d.), p. 30 (Book 3, Chapter 12) and p. 26 (Book 3, Chapter 4).

2. Legge, p. 81 (Book 7, Chapter 9).

3. Legge, pp. 7–8 (Book 1, Chapters 9 and 11).

4. Poo Mu-chou, *In Search of Personal Welfare: A View of Ancient Chinese Religion* (Albany, State University of New York Press, 1998), p. 64.

5. William Theodore de Bary, *Sources of Chinese Tradition* (New York, Columbia University Press, [1960] 1964), Vol. 1, p. 49.

6. De Bary 1964, Vol. 1, pp. 75–6.

7. See illustration in 'Strange Sights Ancient and Modern', Ming woodblock in Frances Wood, *Chinese Illustration* (London, British Library, 1985), p. 36.

8. For the association with Daoism see Ying-shih Yu, 'Life and Immortality in Han China', *Harvard Journal of Asiatic Studies*, 1964–5, Vol. 25, p. 97, and also Joseph Needham, *Science and Civilization in China*, Vol. 2, *The History of Scientific Thought* (Cambridge, Cambridge University Press, 1956), pp. 33–164; and for the corrective view, Timothy Barrett, 'Postscript', in Denis Twitchett and Michael Loewe (eds.), *The Cambridge History of China*, Vol. 1, *The Ch'in and Han Empires 221 BC–AD 220* (Cambridge, Cambridge University Press, 1986), p. 873.

9. Jan Fontein and Ting Wu, *Unearthing China's Past* (Boston, Museum of Fine Arts, 1973), p. 41.

10. K. C. Chang, *The Archaeology of Ancient China*, 4th edition (New Haven, Yale University Press, 1986), pp. 372–4.

11. Lothar von Falkenhausen, 'Sources of Taoism: Reflections on Archaeological Indicators of Religious Change in Eastern Zhou China', *Taoist Resources*, 1994, Vol. 5, No. 2, p. 4.

12. Von Falkenhausen 1994, p. 5.

13. Valerie Hansen, *The Open Empire: A History of China to 1600* (New York, Norton, 2000), pp. 119–21.

14. Donald Harper, 'Resurrection in Warring States Popular Religion', *Taoist Resources*, 1994, Vol. 5, No. 2, pp. 22 and 14.

15. 'Valuable Relics Unearthed in a Tomb at Leigudun', in *Recent Discoveries in Chinese Archaeology* (Beijing, Foreign Languages Press, 1984), pp. 17–21.

16. William H. Nienhauser Jnr, *The Grand Scribe's Records* (Bloomington, Indiana University Press, 1994), Vol. VII, p. 155.

17. Lothar Ledderose, ' A Magic Army for the Emperor', in Lothar Ledderose, *Ten Thousand Things: Module and Mass Production in Chinese Art* (Princeton, Princeton University Press, 2000), p. 55.

18. Ledderose 2000, p. 56.

19. Ladislaw Kesner, 'The Terracotta Army near the First Emperor's Mausoleum', in Xiaoneng Yang, *The Golden Age of Chinese Archaeology: Celebrated Discoveries from the People's Republic of China* (New Haven, Yale University Press, 1999), p. 368.

20. William Watson, *The Genius of China* (London, Royal Academy of Arts, 1973), p. 100.

21. Arthur Cotterell, *The First Emperor of China* (London, Papermac, 1981), pp. 21–2.

22. Maxwell K. Hearn, 'The Terracotta Army of the First Emperor of Qin (221–206 BC)', in Wen Fong, *The Great Bronze Age of China: An Exhibition from the People's Republic of China* (New York, Metropolitan Museum of Art, 1980), pp. 362–3.

23. Hearn 1980, pp. 363–7.

24. Ledderose 2000, p. 69.

25. Ledderose 2000, p. 72.

26. Ledderose 2000, pp. 72–3.

27. Hearn 1980, p. 370, fig. 127.

28. Yuan Zhongyi, *Qin bingmayongkeng* (Beijing, Wenwu chubanshe, 2003), p. 190.

29. Yuan 2003, pp. 194–5.

30. Mark Edward Lewis, 'Warring States Political History', in Michael Loewe and Edward L. Shaughnessy (eds.), *The Cambridge History of Ancient China: From the Origins of Civilization to 221 BC* (Cambridge, Cambridge University Press, 1999), p. 624.

31. Lewis in Loewe and Shaughnessy 1999, p. 625. There is a rather dotty book that attempts to find some sort of Da Vinci code in the Buried Army. In it the hairstyles of the figures are purported to represent solar winds or sun spots, and the knots or joins in the armour are thought to reveal numerical codes if read as a sort of Braille message (not really acknowledging the fact that the ceramic artisans of the Qin didn't know English, let alone English Braille): see Maurice Cotterell, *The Terracotta Warriors: The Secret Codes of the Emperor's Army* (London, Headline, 2003), pp. 138–9.

32. *Qin Shi huangdi bingmayong* (Beijing, Wenwu chubanshe, 1983) [English summary], p. 10

33. *Qin Shi huangdi bingmayong* 1983 [English summary], p. 11.

34. Hearn 1980, p. 367.

35. Yuan 2003, p. 204.

36. Yuan 2003, p. 204; for an illustration, see May Holdsworth, *Warriors of Ancient China* (Hong Kong, FormAsia, 2004), pp. 34–5.

37. Yuan 2003, p. 203: for illustrations, see Corinne Debaine-Francfort, *The Search for Ancient China* (London, Thames and Hudson, 1999), pp. 88 and 96–7.

38. Kesner in Yang 1999, p. 369.

Chapter 12

1. Li Yu-ning, *The First Emperor of China: The Politics of Historiography* (White Plains, International Arts and Sciences Press, 1975), pp. xvii–xviii.

2. Li Yu-ning 1975, pp. xxv–xxvi. Guo's pretentious polymathy can be seen in his scattering of Western references in such pronouncements as '*Wo tebie xihuan Spinoza yinwei wo ai tade pantheism*' / '我特别喜欢 Spinoza 因为我爱她的 pantheism' 'I specially like Spinoza because I love his pantheism'.

3. Li Yu-ning 1975, p. xlix.

4. Translated by the Foreign Languages Press, Beijing, from www.marxists.org/reference/archive/mao/selected-works/poem. Han Wudi (ruled 141–87 BC) was not the first Han emperor, but he was one of the greatest, extending Chinese control into the Gansu corridor out across the north-western deserts; Tang Taizong (ruled AD 627–49), the second Tang emperor, was also considered to be amongst the greatest rulers of that dynasty; Song Taizu had re-established imperial rule in AD 960 after a period of disunion, and Genghis Khan (1167–1227), the great Mongol ruler, paved the way for the Mongol conquest of China in 1276.

5. I have taken the figure of 300,000 from Jonathan Spence, *The Search for Modern China* (New York and London, Norton, 1990), p. 572.

6. Mao's figure is surely simply a multiplication of the First Emperor's supposed burial of the scholars as reported by the Grand Scribe. Kenneth Lieberthal (ed.), *Governing China: From Revolution through Reform* (New York, Norton, 1995), p. 71.

7. Li Yu-ning 1975, p. xlix.

8. The position of Mao's 'heir-apparent' was not a comfortable one. In 1959, Mao had designated Liu Shaoqi as head of the Chinese Communist Party but he was disgraced in 1966 at the very start of the Cultural Revolution and died in prison in 1969. In that same year, Lin Biao was designated as successor. It is interesting to note that Zhou Enlai always managed to avoid nomination and was able to survive, relatively unscathed by personal attacks, until his death from cancer in January 1976. Without wishing to follow Guo Moruo in psychoanalysis of Chairman Mao, I presume that jealousy and unwillingness either to share power or face the fact that a designated 'heir' raised the uncomfortable prospect of his own death formed part of Mao's motivation regarding the effective elimination of his 'heirs'. Though he didn't actually eliminate Lin Biao, the flight towards Moscow must have been provoked by a feeling that the game was up.

9. Stuart Schram (ed.), *Mao Tse-tung Unrehearsed: Talks and Letters 1956–1971*, trans. John Chinnery and Tieyun (Harmondsworth, Penguin, 1975), p. 217.

10. Roderick MacFarquhar and Michael Schoenhals, *Mao's Last Revolution* (Cambridge, Mass., Bellknap Press, 2006), p. 14.

11. Schram 1975, p. 260.

12. MacFarquhar and Schoenhals 2006, p. 367.

13. MacFarquhar and Schoenhals 2006, pp. 367–8.

14. D. C. Lau, *Confucius: The Analects* (Harmondsworth, Penguin, 1979), p. 53.

15. Lau 1979, p. 103. The chair, sometimes referred to as a 'barbarian bed', did not arrive in China until the tenth century AD: see C. P. Fitzgerald, *Barbarian Beds: The Origin*

of the Chair in China (London, Cresset Press, 1965), p. 1. The Chinese term for 'chairman' as in Chairman Mao actually means 'chief mat'. Chairman Mao might have thought of changing or modernizing it, for in its reference to an old cultural habit, it smacks of the 'four olds'.

16. Li Yu-ning 1975, pp. lii–liii.

17. Li Yu-ning 1975, p. lii.

18. Li Yu-ning 1975, p. 214.

19. MacFarquhar and Schoenhals 2006, p. 372.

20. Li Yu-ning 1975, p. 146.

21. A glance at the Internet shows that Sunzi was taken up by management experts in the late 1990s: see To Excel and Zhou Sandou (presumably pseudonyms), *Sunzi's Art of War and Management Strategy* (Lincold, iuniverse.com, 1998), and Mark McNeilly, *Sun Tzu and the Art of Business: Six Strategic Principles for Managers* (New York, Oxford University Press, 1996) (the latter with a final dedication to God, who makes things possible).

22. Li Yu-ning 1975, p. 148.

23. Li Yu-ning 1975, pp. 204–5.

24. Li Yu-ning 1975, pp. 162–3.

25. Li Yu-ning 1975, pp. 180–90.

26. MacFarquhar and Schoenhals 2006, pp. 588, note 38, and 402–4.

27. James R. Pusey, *Wu Han: Attacking the Present through the Past* (Cambridge, Mass., Harvard University Press, 1969) (*Harvard East Asian Monographs 33*), p. x.

28. Arthur F. Wright, *The Sui Dynasty: The Unification of China AD 581–617* (New York, Knopf, 1978), p. 12.

29. Anita M. Andrew and John A. Rapp, *Autocracy and China's Rebel Founding Emperors: Comparing Chairman Mao and Ming Taizu* (Lanham, Rowman and Littlefield, 2000), p. 9. For Zhu Yuanzhang, see L. Carrington Goodrich and Chaoying Fang, *Dictionary of Ming Biography, 1368–1644* (New York, Columbia University Press, 1976), Vol. 1, pp. 381–92.

30. There is a translation of one of the later editions by Nadine Perront, *Wu Han, L'Empereur des Ming* (Arles, Picquier Poche, 1996).

31. There is a fine essay on the Chinese attitude to the past in Simon Leys, *L'Humeur, l'honneur, l'horreur: essais sur la culture et la politique chinoises* (Paris, Laffont, 1991), pp. 11–48.

32. *Qin Shi huangdi bingmayong* (Beijing, Wenwu chubanshe, 1983), p. 1.

Chronology

Xia	21st century BC–c. 1600 BC
Shang	c. 1600–1045 BC
Zhou	Western Zhou 1045–771 BC
	Eastern Zhou 770–256 BC
	Spring and Autumn period 720–476 BC
	Warring States period 475–221 BC
Qin	221–206 BC
Han	Western (or Former) Han 206 BC–AD 23
	Eastern (or Later) Han AD 25–220
Three Kingdoms	Wei AD 220–65
	Shu 221–63
	Wu 222–80
Western Jin	265–316
Eastern Jin	317–420
Northern and Southern States	420–581
Sui	581–618
Tang	618–907
Five Dynasties & Ten Kingdoms	907–79
Song	960–1279

Liao	907–1125
Western Xia	1032–1227
Jin	1115–1234
Yuan	1279–1368
Ming	1368–1644
Qing	1644–1911
Republic	1912–49
People's Republic	1949–

Index